reckson Tada

with the tiniest details of your existence. So learn how his constant pre-
rspective, and healing into the puzzling and chaotic circumstances of
powerful devotional insights.

Joni Eareckson Tada

GLORIOUS INTRUDER

God's Presence in Life's Chaos

MULTNOMAH

Portland, Oregon 97266

Unless otherwise indicated, all Scripture references are from the Holy Bible: New International Version, copyright 1973, 1978, 1984 by the International Bible Society. Used by permission of Zondervan Bible Publishers.

Scripture references marked TLB are from The Living Bible, copyright 1971 by Tyndale House Publishers, Wheaton, Ill. Used by permission.

Scripture references marked NASB are from the New American Standard Bible, copyright The Lockman Foundation, 1960, 1962, 1963, 1968, 1971, 1972, 1973, 1975, 1977. Used by permission.

Scripture references marked KJV are from the King James Version.

Cover design by Bruce DeRoos
Illustrations by Joni Eareckson Tada

Edited by Larry R. Libby

GLORIOUS INTRUDER
© 1989 by Joni Eareckson Tada
Published by Multnomah Press
Portland, Oregon 97266

Multnomah Press is a ministry of Multnomah School of the Bible, 8435 N.E. Glisan Street, Portland, Oregon 97220

Printed in U. S. A.

Library of Congress Cataloging-in-Publication Data

Tada, Joni Eareckson.
   Glorious intruder : God's presence—in lifes chaos / Joni Eareckson Tada.
      p.   cm.
   Bibliography: p.
   Includes index.
   ISBN 0-88070-313-X
   1. Providence and government of God. 2. Christian life—1960-
I. Title.
BT135.T33   1989
231.7—dc20   89-33134
                                                                   CIP

89   90   91   92   93   94   95   96   97   98   -   10   9   8   7   6   5   4   3   2   1

D E D I C A T I O N

For
Jamie Kay Trombero
and Carol Tada

When God intrudes,
may you always see it as glorious.

C O N T E N T S

1

WAITING

Trusting a God Who Lives Beyond Time

21

2

PRAISE

A Thankful Heart in a World of Hurt

47

3

OBEDIENCE

Coming Back to His Control

71

4

FOCUS

Looking to Jesus When Life Gets Confused

97

5

TRUST

Relying On God's Control When Things Fall Apart

121

6

SUFFERING

When God's Gifts Come Wrapped in Pain

143

A C K N O W L E D G E M E N T S

A Special Thanks To. . .

The staff of Joni and Friends—for being part of the team who helped pray this book into being.

Bev Singleton, Francie Lorey, and **Kati Peterson**—some of the fastest typing fingers in the West. A special thanks to Francie, who organized so much material and proofed and re-proofed the manuscript.

Al Sanders and **Carl Miller**—our friends at Ambassador Agency, tireless cheerleaders in helping Joni and Friends get our message out.

The **Reverend Gregory Hotchkiss**—a fine writer from the Reformed Episcopal Church who started me thinking about the way God intrudes in our lives. . . at the most unlikely times. I'm grateful for his wisdom and scholarship.

Multnomah Press—my friends, my publishing family. And special thanks to **Brenda Jose** for caring so much about the look and feel of my book.

Larry Libby—editor and unsung hero behind this book.

I N T R O D U C T I O N

God is an intruder.

He encroaches, presumes, invades, and infringes. He crashes the party. Tears aside curtains. Throws open locked doors. Hits the light switch in a dark room. God pulls the fire alarm in stuffy, sacrosanct hallways.

He intruded primeval chaos and brought forth light, beauty, order, and life.

He presumed upon the life of a middle-aged man in the town of Ur, and brought forth a nation.

He trespassed on the cozy security of the Canaanites, smug behind their walls of stone.

He advanced upon the lofty chambers of kings with finger-wagging, feisty old prophets who called down judgment.

He was the unwelcomed guest at Belshazzar's feast, writing doom on the wall while the revelers gagged on their wine.

God intruded the womb of a virgin. He stormed Satan's kingdom on a Christmas night in Bethlehem. He talked out of turn in Judah and Galilee with words that "no man spoke before." He crashed the temple courtyards, overturning tables and kicking commerce out the door with a strong arm and a whip of cords.

God overstepped the realm of death itself, stealing its banner and crushing its lord. And in the Most Holy Place of the temple, He audaciously tore the veil from top to bottom.

And in the end, He will once again intervene in history, judging the nations, banishing sin and death, and setting His throne upon earth even as He rules heaven.

God is a glorious intruder in my life, my thoughts, my pain, sorrow, and brokenness.

The Spirit of the Lord even invades *me,* taking up residence in my very body. His Word is a razor-edged sword, piercing my complacency and dividing my soul and spirit. He boldly intrudes into my sin, brashly calling it what it is, challenging me to leave it behind.

What can we do but marvel in speechless wonder at our powerful and Almighty God—who, incidentally, has every right to intrude? After all, can the owner of the house really "intrude" when he sets foot inside his own door? Can a king be tabbed "interfering" when he visits the subjects of his own realm? Can a craftsman be thought a "trespasser" when he wraps his fingers around his own stick of wood?

God, an intruder? From His perspective, never. From our point of view? It happens all the time. Whether He encroaches with a gentle, subtle reminder or in sudden, devastating judgment.

And that's why I've written this book—so that you may see more of how God intrudes upon your life every day. So you can wonder at it, revel in it, and be gloriously blessed by the fact that your God cares enough to step into your life . . . sometimes when you least expect it.

We dare not think that God is absent or daydreaming. The do-nothing God. He's not tucked away in some far corner of the universe, uncaring, unfeeling, unthinking . . . uninvolved. Count on it—God intrudes in glorious and myriad ways.

And thank His holy Name He does!

WAITING

Trusting a God
Who Lives Beyond Time

WAITING
Trusting a God
Who Lives Beyond Time

God, are you there?

Silence.

Are you listening?

More silence.

Ummm . . . am I getting the idea that You're asking me to wait? Is that what I'm supposed to do? Just—sit here and WAIT?

A very long silence.

Why is it, God, that when I want to charge ahead, You insist I wait? And at other times—when I feel like waiting—You push me forward?

Deafening silence.

You had hoped God wouldn't do this. Not now, not at this time, not in this situation. But He has. And it's exasperating. He replies to your questions with long, drawn-out periods of silence. No answers, no directions, no warm fuzzies, no road sign pointing, "This is the way, walk ye in it." Just . . . waiting.

Okay. If I have to sit here and wait, then I'll . . . I'll. . . .

Before you know it, you've created your own noise, activity, and excitement—anything but that grating stillness which seems to rub against the grain of your soul.

It's a common problem. We frantically crowd our time with more frenzy, hoping to satisfy our soul's longings. We do spiritual frog-hops from one activity to the next . . .

sign up for an extra committee at church . . .

agree to accept the chairman position . . .

volunteer in the nursery . . .

arrange for the Bible study's potluck dinner . . .

count the offering after every worship service . . .

offer to help with the junior Sunday school class . . .

And what does all this get us? Spiritual exhaustion. Mental burnout. Physical drain. And even a few more irksome feelings about God.

Oswald Chambers has observed, "When we are in an unhealthy state physically or emotionally, we always want thrills. And in the spiritual domain, if we insist on getting thrills, on mounting up with wings, it will end in the destruction of spirituality."[1]

But I'm tired of waiting! you say.

Ah, the Spirit of Christ hasn't forgotten you. He's listening. Finally you heave a deep sigh. *I'm at the end of my rope. I yield to You, Lord.*

The Spirit is working.

Ignoring your frenzy, bypassing your busyness, the Glorious Intruder quietly elbows His way into your activity, whispering, "Be still and know that I am God."

Even though you have a hard time believing that any worthwhile activity can exist in stillness, God begins to do His hushed work in your heart. He gives you His inexplicable calm as you wait by the hospital bed of your husband. He gives you patience as you wait for the letter of acceptance from college. Peace as you wait for the job opportunity. And more than that, He gives you Himself, His intimacy, as you search for an answer to your deepest longings. It dawns on you that rush is wrong nearly every time.

It's a command; it's a charge: "Keep silence before Me . . . and let the people renew their strength" (Isaiah 41:1, KJV).

It's a bidding, a mandate: "Be silent, all mankind, before the Lord" (Zechariah 2:13, TLB).

When we do, when we are—wonder of wonders!—we hear "a still, small voice." God's answer comes only through waiting.

THE OTHER SIDE OF THE SCALE

The sufferings of this present time are not worthy to be compared with the glory which shall be revealed in us (Romans 8:18, KJV).

When someone first showed me that verse in the hospital many years ago, I thought, *Great. What's the Bible doing? Telling me my problems with paralysis are featherweight?*

At first I thought the writer was making light of my suffering, telling me to "cheer up and not be depressed." I thought this verse was dismissing my troubles casually, and that my load, from a biblical perspective, should be considered no big deal. Instead of being comforted, I felt choked with resentment.

That may have been a young, stubborn teenager's way of looking at that verse, but the Bible doesn't speak carelessly or flippantly when it says today's sufferings aren't worthy to be compared with the glory yet to be. Nor is it trying to make molehills out of our mountainous problems.

What could be more cruel than making light of someone's anguish? The disappointments and grief we sometimes experience are painfully real, and it is a false comforter who says, "What are you complaining about? Buck up, it'll all work out."

But God's Word is no false comforter. To help us gain perspective on this verse, Martyn Lloyd-Jones offered a simple word picture. Imagine, he said, a man sitting at a table with a pair of scales before him. On one side of the scales are his sufferings. The man looks at them and sees they are very heavy. But then he looks on the other side of the scale, filling his vision with the much heavier weight of the glory yet to be. And what seemed so heavy before appears now to be as light as a feather. It's not that his sufferings are light in themselves, they only *become* light in contrast to the far greater weight on the other side of the scale.

All this sounded like nice theory as I lay on my back in that hospital bed. The wonder of Romans 8:18 came only *after* I forced myself to be realistic and face my troubles as they were—at their worst. Then, when I felt I could no longer bear the pressure, I looked at the other side. I took a long, hard look at the glory yet to be revealed.

And what will this glory be? C. S. Lewis probably came as close as anyone to putting it into words:

> We are to shine as the sun, we are to be given the Morning Star . . . in one way, of course, God has given us the Morning Star already: You can go and enjoy the gift on many fine mornings if you get up early enough. What more, you may ask, do we want? . . . We want something else which can hardly be put into words— to be united with the beauty we see, to pass into it, to receive it unto ourselves, to bathe in it, to become part of it . . . Yet, at present we are on the outside of the world, the wrong side of the door. We discern the freshness and purity of morning, but they do not make us fresh and pure. We cannot mingle with the splendors we see. But all the leaves of the New Testament are rustling with the rumor that it will not always be so. Someday, God willing, we shall get *in*. When human souls have become as perfect in voluntary obedience, then they will put on its glory, or rather that greater glory of which Nature is only the first sketch. Nature is mortal; we shall outlive her. When all the suns and nebulae have passed away, each one of you will still be alive. Nature is only the image, the symbol; but it is the symbol Scripture invites me to use. We are summoned to pass in through Nature, beyond her, into that splendor which she fitfully reflects.[2]

For me, an artist who loves sunsets and moonrises and cold starlight between pine trees in the high Sierras, this language offers a glimpse, a passing glance, at the weight of glory which will far outweigh today's heartaches.

In the very next verse, Paul seems to speak of a craning-your-neck, standing-on-tip-toe way of peering through the mists at the wonders to come.

The creation waits in eager expectation for the sons of
God to be revealed (v. 19).

The best we can hope for in this life is a knothole peek at the
shining realities ahead. Yet a glimpse is enough. It's enough to
convince our hearts that whatever sufferings and sorrows cur-
rently assail us aren't worthy of comparison to that which waits
over the horizon.

Yes, there are those times when you can't help but consider
your present circumstances; when, with a sigh, you find yourself
gazing at the heavy load on your side of the scale. Go ahead and
look.

But don't leave your eyes there too long. There's another
side to that scale. Fill the eyes of your heart with what's waiting
on the other side of eternity.

You'll find there is no comparison.

PRESENT-TENSE FAITH

"Have faith, Joni . . . one day it will all be better."

I can't tell you how many times I heard words like those from sad-faced friends who clung to the guardrail of my hospital bed when I was first injured.

"Have faith, Joni . . . faith will see you through to the end."

Boy, that sounded morbid to me.

I could never be comforted by words like those. They always left me with a feeling that nothing much was *really* going to change. My paralysis was still to be a prison, and faith—a kind of hopeful, wistful longing—was only a religious warm fuzzy to cheer me until a faraway, future day when everything would "make sense."

If being a woman of great faith meant sitting around in my wheelchair longing for pie in the sky, I wanted no part of it.

What a colossal misunderstanding!

Faith, as the Bible defines it, is present-tense action. It's taking God's promises and acting on them *today*. This "right now" way of looking at God's assurances is the stuff of which great people of faith are made. They simply take God at His Word and live on that basis. To them, faith is pulled out of the abstract, out of the nebulous nowhere, out of the syrupy twilight, and lived with concrete certainty in the here and now.

Somewhere along the line I realized that. On some dark night in a sterile room the words of Hebrews 11:1 began to seep through my stubborn defenses. I began to realize that faith means being sure of what we hope for . . . *now*. It means knowing something is real, *this moment*, all around you, even when you don't see it.

When I started living like this, I suddenly understood I could get a jump-start on heaven. I could start living for eternity today. I could have confidence that God had His busy fingers working on me moment by moment, even though I couldn't see or feel them.

Great faith isn't the ability to believe long and far into the misty future. It's simply taking God at His word and taking the next step.

WE MAY ASK WHY

If the Lord Jesus cried out on His cross, "My God, my God, why have you forsaken me?" is it okay for me to ask the question "Why?"

I wondered that for the longest time. My cries of "why God, why?" weren't voiced out of anger. For the most part it was a human cry, a cry of desperation out of my own agony.

Over the years I've discovered it's no sin to ask the Lord why things happen. God can handle our questions. But here's the important thing: *Can we handle His answers?*

Yes, there are answers. So many of us get so caught up in asking "why me?" we may forget about seeking those answers. The fact is, we may not like them. They may be hard to swallow. But we can't ignore the fact that God can and does give crystal clear answers to our heart's deepest questions.

So why does God allow the hurt you're facing today?

You might find part of your answer in the words of Peter:

Dear friends, do not be surprised at the painful trial you are suffering, as though something strange were happening to you. But rejoice that you participate in the sufferings of Christ, so that you may be overjoyed when his glory is revealed (1 Peter 4:12-13).

You see, part of the answer to the "whys" you are asking might be that God wants you to have a small share in the sort of suffering your Savior went through.

Paul echoes a similar thought:

Now if we are children, then we are heirs—heirs of God and co-heirs with Christ, if indeed we share in his sufferings in order that we may also share in his glory (Romans 8:17).

Once again God gives us at least a partial answer to our "why" questions. It's almost as though God is saying to us *"Why not?"* If Jesus went through so much . . . so much suffering and heartache to secure for us that which we don't deserve . . . if He went through the pain, should we complain if we have to endure a tiny part of what He went through on our behalf?

The Bible makes it clear that suffering is somehow intimately linked with the glory that lies beyond. The 1 Peter 4 and Romans 8 passages remind us we can rejoice over the privilege of participating in the sufferings of Christ so that we will be overjoyed when we share in His glory to come.

Now, that may not be the kind of answer we want or expect to the questions we ask of God. But God's not the one who has to prove Himself here.

You've been more than ready to ask the questions. The real issue is, will you accept His answers?

The Thing about Greener Grass

Lot looked out across Canaan's prime real estate, the beautiful Jordan Valley.

Not a bad place to put down roots, he probably thought. Rich, well-watered grazing land. Fertile fields. Good, dark soil. And grass as green as a valley full of emeralds.

The tribes of Lot and his kindly uncle Abram were having problems living in the same neighborhood, so the older man graciously told his nephew to set up camp wherever he liked.

> Abram said to Lot, "Let's not have any quarreling between you and me . . . Is not the whole land before you? Let's part company. If you go to the left, I'll go to the right; if you go to the right, I'll go to the left" (Genesis 13:8-9).

Scripture tells us that the young man lifted his gaze across the green river valley and "chose for himself the whole plain of the Jordan and set out toward the east" (v. 11).

Yes, the grass was green, and the Jordan sparkled in the sunlight. But little did Lot know there were some built-in problems to that valley. Strange people with weird customs. Cities full of crime and violence and sexual perversions. Deadly thorns and stinging nettles nestled on the wide, green bosom of the plain. The hidden price tag of Lot's hot real estate deal—the prime land just outside Sodom and Gomorrah—bore the names of his own family.

When you think about it, you and I aren't all that different from our friend Lot, are we? Like you, I tend to choose the easy course of action, the smooth path of progress. *If it looks good and there are no hitches, then this must be the way God wants me to go.* Then, if I don't run into any hardships or tough problems, I make the judgment that I'm experiencing God's blessing.

But, oh, when the going gets tough—when the thorns and thistles rear their pointy heads to block my path—I wonder just what God has in mind. And sure enough, I start looking back and second-guessing myself. I start dwelling on all the "could-have-beens" and "might-have-beens."

My mistake is in thinking the grass is greener simply because the path looks so easy. The fact is, *there is no greener grass elsewhere.* Those first impressions of the "easier path" simply don't tell the whole story. If we're following the course God has placed before us, we will have thorns and thistles wherever we go. Oh sure, there will be plenty of beautiful green vistas and sunlit fields along the way to make our journey pleasant. But Scripture makes it clear that we can also count on our fair share of problems and pain. God will make certain of that, so that we'll make certain we stick close to Him every step of the way.

The only greener grass I know of is in heaven. It's a place where there are no thorns or thistles, problems or heartaches. A place of real peace and lasting joy with our Savior, our friends and family, and the saints of all ages.

So if you're tempted to think life ought to be better someplace else—maybe with a new set of circumstances, a new job, a new city, or a new mate—believe me, the grass you're imagining isn't always that green. Only in heaven will life be as good and great as you'd like it to be.

Don't let the devil tell you otherwise. If his grass looks greener, it's only because it's artificial turf.

"Are We There Yet?"

When I was little, I'd love it when the whole family would pile into the station wagon and head off to Uncle Doug and Aunt Fran's dairy farm up in northeast Maryland.

All of us kids loved Uncle Doug. He let us milk the cows and feed them grain. It was so much fun to reach out and pet the soft, wet muzzle of a cow munching away on her cud. The barn brimmed with hay where we could build forts and throw straw. And out in the back acres it was "Tomato Wars" with big, juicy, overripe tomatoes.

We'd be in trouble, of course, when we'd come into the farmhouse for dinner, all covered with tomato. But it was all part of the fun.

It really wasn't that far to Uncle Doug's in the car—maybe only fifty miles. But for some reason the trip seemed to take *forever*. Not more than fifteen minutes into the drive, we would lean over the front seat and whine, "Are we there yet? When are we gonna get there?" and "Why is it taking so long?"

That memory came back to me recently when I was studying the book of Numbers in the Bible. Freshly released from four centuries of slavery in Egypt, the Israelites were filled with visions of the Promised Land. What a home it would be! Freedom . . . elbow room . . . and what was it God had said? A land "flowing with milk and honey"? It sounded too good to be true.

Thoughts of that beautiful country to the north must have filled their imaginations those first mornings as they would break camp, pack up, and wait for the trumpet to signal another day's march. But just three days into the journey, the Bible tells us they began to murmur and complain.

I can just picture them saying to Moses and Aaron, "Are we there yet? When are we gonna get there? Why is it taking so long?"

They must have made the trip miserable for Moses, who knew they had quite a long way to go. And much like us kids when we were little, they lacked patience and self-control. They despised the long wait and the boredom of plodding along at what they felt was a very slow pace.

Could it be the same for you and me when we think about heaven, our Promised Land? Does the bright picture of our future Home make us bored and unsatisfied with our lot down here on earth? Do we impatiently think to ourselves, *When are we ever going to get there? Why is it taking so long?* In our lack of perseverance and discipline, do we complain about what seems to be a long wait?

Let's not be like spoiled children. And let's certainly not be like those grumblers in the desert who brought distress to their leaders and grief and anger to their God.

No, the very idea of a Promised Land to come, of heaven yet to be, should fill our hearts with joy and inspire us onward in the journey with strength and real patience.

Are we there yet?

No, not yet. Not quite. But every day brings us closer.

When are we going to get there?

In His time. At the best time. Perhaps sooner than we would expect.

Why is it taking so long?

Our loving God must want us Home more than we want to be Home. Yet there is work to do, people to reach, and a Savior to follow down the winding road of days and years.

When we finally turn into heaven's driveway and see Him waiting at the open door, the long drive won't seem so long at all.

HEAVEN: CATCHING UP WITH OUR HEART

Some people find it difficult to think realistically about heaven.

Even Christians feel awkward working toward "eternity," simply because, well . . . it seems so far away, almost unreal. Something between a Sunday School paper sketch and a half-remembered dream. Even when we try to imagine what it will be like, we come up short of a real desire to go there. Heaven is supposed to be a *place*, not simply a state of mind; but try as we may, it's tough to picture it.

It's little wonder we feel so blasé about it all. The image most people concoct about heaven is anything but appealing. Some imagine it a spooky kind of twilight zone. Others visualize it tucked behind a galaxy where birds chirp and organs play with heavy tremolo and angels bounce from cloud to cloud.

If *that* were a true picture of heaven, I'd be lukewarm about going there, too.

But the fact is that we believers are headed for heaven. It's reality. Heaven may be as near as next year—or next week. So it makes good sense to spend some time here on earth thinking candid thoughts about that future reserved for us.

I admit, it's tough to muster excitement about a place we've never seen. So how do we go about bringing heaven into focus?

Someone once said that Christ brings the heart to heaven first—and then He brings the person. I like that. God knows you and I would have a tough time fixing our eyes on heaven unless our heart was really involved. That's why our Lord's words in Matthew 6:21 rings so true: "For where your treasure is, there will your heart be also" (KJV).

In other words, if our investments are in heaven, God knows our heart's desire will be there, too.

I'm convinced this little verse in Matthew 6 holds the secret. The only way we can enjoy the thought of heaven, the only way we can start thinking of it as reality, is to allow God to take our heart home first. Once we start investing in eternity, heaven will begin to come into focus. As we give sacrificially of our energies or money, as we spend more time in prayer, praising God rather than petitioning Him, as we witness boldly and fearlessly . . . we're making deposits in eternity. We're putting more and more of *ourselves* on the other side. As we continue to do these things, we'll wake up one morning to find our heart precisely where it should be . . . in heaven.

Our future Home won't seem like an eerie twilight zone. It won't fill our thoughts with saccharine visions of bluebirds, chubby angels, and rainbows. No, it will take shape in our minds as the *Real* Estate it actually is, the place where God dwells, and prepares for our coming.

"Your eyes will see the king in his beauty and view a land that stretches afar" (Isaiah 33:17). All the other trappings—golden streets, pearly gates, and crystal rivers—aren't nearly as important.

What *is* important is that we will see our King and live with Him forever. In that shining moment we will finally catch up with our hearts—and our heart's desire.

God Himself.

And that will be enough.

WAITING

Most of my disabled friends would agree that one of the hardest disciplines any of us must grapple with is patience. It's one of those lessons we have to relearn every day, many times over.

On the mornings that Ken teaches, for instance, a friend comes to our house to do my morning routine and see me off to work. Often my friend will say something like "What a lovely day!" Or, "I don't think it's going to be nearly as hot today as it was yesterday."

When I hear comments like that, I want to bounce out of bed, head for the back yard, and appraise the day for myself. I want to breathe some of that fresh morning air. I want to see my roses while they're still covered with dew.

But it's simply not possible. My morning routine—including exercises and bathing—chews up an hour or more before I can even get into my wheelchair. So be patient, I must!

It's during such moments of waiting I think of all that has to be done. Do you identify with that? Sitting in the waiting (!) room at the doctor's office you remember half a dozen phone calls you need to make. Parked in a long line of stop-and-go traffic on the freeway you think of all the stuff you need to pick up at the market on the way home—and the time is getting late.

It's a fact. Waiting is not an easy thing to do.

I've spent so much of my time waiting in a bed or waiting in a wheelchair. After my diving injury, I waited to be moved from the intensive care unit into a regular hospital room. After three months of waiting there, I was finally moved to a rehabilitation center. While in rehab, I waited every day to go to occupational and physical therapy. In the evenings, I'd wait for friends or family to come in for a visit. And it seemed as though I was waiting *forever* to go home.

Waiting. Unfortunately, most of us associate the word with phrases like "hanging around" or "killing time." We get a mental picture of leaning up against a wall with our arms folded, yawning, occasionally glancing at our watch.

But there's far more to waiting than lounging around until we receive what we hope for. George Matheson wrote insightfully about the *manner* in which we should wait.

> We commonly associate patience with lying down. We think of it as the angel that guards the couch of the invalid. Yet there is a patience that I believe to be harder—the patience that can run. To lie down in the time of grief, to be quiet under the stroke of adverse fortune, implies a great strength. But I know of something that implies a strength greater still. It is the power to work under stress, to continue under hardship, to have anguish in your spirit and still perform daily tasks. This is a Christlike thing. The hardest thing is that most of us are called to exercise patience, not in the sick bed, but in the street.

Waiting is something more than "counting flowers on the wall," as the old song goes. It takes *courage* to live out our patience on the street, to wait and yet still remain active and involved.

"Wait on the Lord," Psalm 27:14 tells us, "be of good courage" (KJV). Those times we find ourselves having to wait on others may be perfect opportunities to train ourselves to wait on the Lord. Instead of fidgeting and fuming, we could use such moments to pull Bible verses out of our memory, or learn more of God's Word. I'm not talking about the mechanical repetition of words, but actually weaving biblical truth into the fabric of our day.

Wait on the Lord in prayer as you sit on the freeway, sharing with Him the anxiety of so many jobs to be done in such a short time. Watch your frustrations melt into praise as you sing hymns and choruses for His ears alone.

By exercising this kind of patience, rooted in God's Word, we can say with the psalmist, "I wait for the Lord, my soul waits, and in his word I put my hope" (Psalm 130:5).

So . . .

if you're single and waiting for marriage...

if you're a preteen and waiting for high school...

if you're stuck in your career and waiting for a break...

if you're parked in a wheelchair and waiting for a push...

if you're married and waiting for your husband to change... make sure you keep *living* while you're waiting.

It takes courage to wait patiently and yet get out there and embrace life. But you can do it. Lean on God and courage will never be in short supply.

APPRECIATING PRAYER

Have you ever wondered how people can spend thousands of dollars on a *painting*, of all things?

Or how someone can stand for twenty minutes in front of a Rembrandt in a museum? Or how folks can ooh and ahh over a sculpture or an Ansel Adams photograph?

Do you ever scratch your head and wonder just what people see in art?

Or take music. Does it puzzle you that people buy season tickets to the symphony—and hardly miss a performance? Why do people listen for hours to Bach? And what's so captivating about a Mendelssohn concerto or a Strauss waltz or a Chopin minuet?

Oh sure, you admit they all have their fine points. Art and music are nice to occasionally dabble in, but, come on—how is it that some people go overboard on such things?

If you feel that way . . . I understand. I used to shrug my shoulders toward art and music, too. I suppose I was lacking what they call "appreciation."

But I also remember when that ho-hum, scratch-your-head attitude began to change. It all started when my art teacher sat down with me and started flipping through pages and pages of art books. At almost every page, he would stop and linger over a Monet print or a Cezanne reproduction. He would spend hours discussing the composition and color in a painting by Mary Cassatt.

At first I felt . . . well, bored. But the more I looked and listened, the more I began to appreciate. Spending time with the masters elevated my thinking. I began to see things I had never seen. The more I looked, the more was revealed, and the more I understood.

Now when I see someone stand for long minutes in front of a Rembrandt, I smile and nod my head. I can identify.

If you don't appreciate good art, then go to a museum and start *looking* at good art. If you don't appreciate fine music, go to a concert and *listen* to fine music.

I know people who have a similar struggle when they look at the prayer habits of others. They listen to someone getting all excited about spending a morning talking to the Lord, and can only shake their heads. They will be the first to admit they simply do not appreciate the work of prayer.

Frankly, the only way you and I can develop a real appreciation for prayer is to pray. Prayer itself is an art which only the Holy Spirit can teach.

Pray for prayer.

Pray to be helped in prayer.

Pray until you appreciate prayer.

Like art, like music, like so many other disciplines, prayer can only be appreciated when you actually spend time in it. Spending time with the Master will elevate your thinking. The more you pray, the more will be revealed. You will understand. You will smile and nod your head as you identify with others who fight long battles and find great joy on their knees.

You will appreciate not only the greatness of prayer, but the greatness of God.

No Easy Road

You've asked your good friend for directions. He obliges with a specific, detailed, hand-drawn map.

Reassured, you set off on your journey only to discover the route he has given you is a jumbled mess. A real nightmare. It's a road full of detours, gaping potholes, puddles, ruts, and ripped-up pavement. Terrible drop-offs loom on the crumbling shoulders of the road, with not a guardrail in sight. Nowhere on that horrible road is there a place to turn around—and you're much too far along to back up!

There you are, bumping along with sharp-edged boulders knifing at your oil pan, scraping your whitewalls, ruining your alignment.

You'd be fuming, wouldn't you?

But what would hurt more than anything is the knowledge that your friend *knew* the road was like that. Most likely you'd pass the time rehearsing what to tell that joker the next time you came nose-to-nose with him.

"Hey, buddy, thanks for nothing! Next time I'll get where I need to go without your help!"

What would you think of a friend like that—one who had deliberately given you those directions and sent you down that dangerous road?

You'd drop him. Fast.

That's what you or I would do. Consider, though, what happened to the apostle Paul. The preacher from Tarsus was given directions that sent him down a more tortured road than the one I've just described—a road of dangers, hunger, humiliation, loneliness, terror, and blood.

Paul received his directions in the middle of the night. In a lonely detention cell. From the mouth of the Lord Himself.

"The following night the Lord stood near Paul and said, 'Take courage! As you have testified about me in Jerusalem, so you must also testify in Rome'" (Acts 23:11).

Okay, so there was the Lord Jesus giving Paul his route.

"The road I want you to take, Paul, is the one that's going to Rome. Keep heading in that direction no matter what. You can't miss it."

With Jesus Himself as travel agent, you'd expect a First Class trip, right? Not so. For two years on that long road to Rome, Paul faced more than his fair share of bypasses, ruts, hazards, and roadblocks. The journey featured constant trouble, murderous plots, and imprisonments. Then there was that long detour when a hurricane tossed him around the Mediterranean for fourteen days. Until his ship finally hit a sandbar.

And broke into pieces.

After which he managed to swim to an island.

After which he was bitten by a poisonous snake.

An easy road? Hey, the Roman Road was no freeway. The tolls were unbelievably high. And yet *this was the very road Jesus told him to take.* Ah, but Paul trusted his Friend. Though the road was rugged—even vicious at times—Paul trusted. He never denied his friendship with Christ.

And when he got to Rome? Oh, how the Lord used him!

You may wish the road Jesus sent you on had a turnaround. Maybe you've even been tempted to shift into reverse and back away from His direction.

Listen. Just take those road hazards—the potholes, ruts, detours, and all the rest—as evidence that you're on the right route.

It's when you find yourself on that big, broad, easy road that you ought to worry.

PRAISE

*A Thankful Heart
in a World of Hurt*

2

PRAISE
A Thankful Heart
in a World of Hurt

Like supernatural effervescence, praise will sometimes
bubble up from the joy of simply knowing Christ. Praise like that
is . . . delight. Pure pleasure!

How can you define the rush of adoring words which flows
from your lips to the throne of God? How can you explain it? It
defies dissection or analysis. Rejoicing in Him is the kind of
praise which speaks for itself!

But praise can also be supernatural determination. A deci-
sive action. Praise like that is . . . quiet resolve. Fixed devotion.
Strength of spirit.

Perhaps this kind of praise needs some explanation.

When we praise God out of quiet determination, it's a

sacrifice. A sacrifice of praise will always cost you something. It will be a difficult thing to do.

Reflect for a moment on the most frightening crises in your life or the life of your family: a cancerous lump, a debilitating illness, a financial emergency, a daughter's illegitimate pregnancy, a son's angry rebellion. If during those times you have steadfastly fastened your heart in praise to God, then you have offered a sacrifice. If with the psalmist you have said to the Lord, "I will always have hope; I will praise you more and more" (Psalm 71:14), you have offered words which have cost you something.

A sacrifice of praise will always be a spendy proposition. It requires trading in our pride, our anger, and most valued of all, our human logic. We will be tempted to think our "intruder" God is overstepping reasonable bounds, asking us to express praise when it seems more rational to express doubt. We will be compelled to voice our words of praise firmly and precisely, even as our logic screams that God has no idea what He's doing.

In Psalm 65:1, David sings, "Praise awaits you, O God . . . to you our vows will be fulfilled." I've been told the Hebrew term translated "await" means "quiet trust." Such a trust could be expressed like this:

I have prayed about this burden, this emergency, and now, Lord, I will deliberately fix my heart on praising You even before I see the answer. The answer to my prayer hasn't come yet, but I expect it. And my praise—a sacrifice—is my offering to You in demonstration of my belief and confidence.

I think that God is especially honored when we offer a sacrifice of praise. He is glorified when we offer words of adoration wrenched from a pained and bruised heart. Perhaps that's because He values the precious weight of each word of praise that's been sacrificed.

Most of the verses written about praise in God's Word were penned by men and women who faced crushing heartaches, injustice, treachery, slander, and scores of other intolerable situations. Little wonder that Hebrews 13:15 reminds us of the value of praising God even when it hurts.

Through Jesus, therefore, let us continually offer to God a sacrifice of praise—the fruit of lips that confess His name.

It is only "through Jesus" that we are able to offer a sacrifice of praise. Why? Because Jesus was God's sacrifice for us. Is it asking too much, then, for us to sacrifice mere words? Never! God is definitely not overstepping reasonable bounds when He asks us to offer a sacrifice of praise.

He has been *more* than generous with us. May we be as generous with our words of praise.

Whatever kind of praise you offer—joyful effervescence or quiet determination—may the thoughts on the following pages help you to fix your praise on Him.

SELF-PITY AT THE DOOR

The modern technology which has brought us so many helpful new products, plastics, insecticides, and preservatives looms like a deadly curse for a friend of mine.

Linda has been chemically poisoned. As a result, she's lost the ability to tolerate this synthetic world of ours.

I went to see her last week at her little place tucked back in the Santa Barbara hills. For two weeks prior, I had to go through a total "detoxification" of my clothes, my body, and my hair. I couldn't use perfumes, deodorants, or soaps. I couldn't even eat garlic or onion or anything spicy.

As we ate together in her home, Linda described an incident from the previous week. She was forced to endure a lengthy confinement in her bedroom simply because the neighbors down the road were having a barbecue. One whiff of wind-blown lighter fluid can cause her to lose consciousness.

Because of her disability, Linda is mostly alone. She is isolated from friends and family. Yet her solitude is often disturbed by a persistent visitor at her door. This unwelcome acquaintance knocks and knocks, whining and pleading to get in.

His name is Self-Pity.

It's certainly easy to understand why Linda feels tempted to let this unrelenting visitor in. It would be easy to feel sorry for herself when she has to use an old-style metal telephone with ancient, deteriorating parts that can't be replaced. Her shouted conversations over that phone leave her frustrated and exhausted.

Does she have it rough? Don't you think she deserves some time off for a few hours visit with Self-Pity? Some people would say yes—and understandably so.

But Linda? Listen to what she told me:

"No, Joni, suffering and sickness and pain don't rank high on my list of best possible options for a happy life. But God alone can determine what's best for me. Only He sees the beginning from the end. He's the only One who knows what it's going to take to conform me to the image of His Son. And He spares no pain in accomplishing His will in my life. I don't need pity; and what I need even less is my own pity."

We all find days when Self-Pity, like an obnoxious sales-man, keeps ringing the bell and pounding on our door. Days when we feel as though nobody has it as tough as we do. You know those days: a dish clatters to the floor, the phone rings, the garbage disposal chokes to death, the automatic garage door opener goes on strike, and the bank informs you that another check just bounced.

Ah, poor me! you think to yourself.

Before you offer hospitality to old Self-Pity, remember Linda in the Santa Barbara hills. Linda who endures so much aloneness, but surrounds herself with the prayers of caring Christian friends . . . and refuses to allow that persistent knocker entrance.

If she can keep that door closed and latched, so can you.

THE DIFFERENCE BETWEEN OUR SUFFERING
. . . AND HIS

It's no use trying to fake it with the staff at Joni and Friends. They've seen me at my worst.

On different occasions I've come into the office downcast, completely disheartened for one reason or another. My friends in our ministry have had the sensitivity to be a real comfort to me. After sharing a few mutual problems and prayer needs, I begin to feel like I honestly *am* a part of the fellowship of suffering.

All Christians participate in that marvelous fellowship. Through the smiles, sharing of struggles, prayerful lifting of burdens, tears, and even the consolation and occasional advice, we are initiated into the fellowship of Christ's sufferings.

For all believers, there is a wonderful, inexplicable participation in the life and power of Jesus when we suffer. Ours is a fellowship in which the power of Jesus is made perfect, not just alongside of or beyond our weaknesses, but actually *in* our weakness. Two of the words most associated with Christians in their suffering are "comfort" and "joy."

But it's right at this point that we need to understand a big difference between *our* suffering and the suffering our Lord went through.

For the Lord Jesus, there was *no* fellowship in suffering.

For the Lord, there was only the wooden insensitivity of His disciples—from the first day right up to the end of His ministry.

For Him, there was only that awful climax of isolation on the cross, even to the point of being forsaken by the Father and abandoned to God's blazing wrath.

There was no real *joy* in His cross as there can be in ours. Hebrews 12:2 tells us that "for the joy *set before Him* He endured the cross." In other words, Jesus focused on that which was beyond those ghastly hours: on His future back with the Father, and on the salvation of millions who would trust Him through history. But thankfully for us, we can have joy *in* our affliction. Right in the heart of it. Ours is a comfort we can experience *now* as we suffer.

For Jesus, it was a different story. Far different.

You don't have to be alone in your hurt! Comfort *is* yours. Joy *is* an option. And it's all been made possible by your Savior. He went without comfort so that you might have it. He post-poned joy so that you might share in it. He willingly chose isolation so that you might never be alone in your hurt and sorrow. He had no real fellowship so that fellowship might be yours, this moment.

So let's you and I drop our martyr complex, okay? You will never experience isolation or abandonment or the dread of being forsaken as did your Lord. You've got fellowship! The fellowship of suffering!

And you have it because He didn't.

PRESENT-DAY MARTYRS

I blew the dust off an old quote the other day. It was in one of those obscure volumes off the top shelf in a back closet—one that would have never made it on the Christian Bestseller list.

The phrase went like this:

The final crown of glory in this world is martyrdom, and the blood of martyrs is the seed of the Church.

Don't hear that kind of talk much these days, do we?

It's not the kind of stuff that draws good ratings on Christian talk shows. That's one quote you'll never see stitched in needlepoint in the family room, or inscribed in gold on a greeting card. Not the sort of phrase likely to end up on a tee-shirt or bumper sticker.

Words like those seem a little musty . . . linked to another age, long ago and far away.

Yet *nothing* was more potent in bringing unbelievers to faith in the early days of the Church than the witness of suffering believers. Even when Christians were beaten, abused, condemned to death, and thrown to the lions, the world was astounded to witness them thanking their God that they had been counted worthy to suffer shame for His Name.

Nothing has shaken unbelievers—then and now—as the way believers endure hardship. What, they ask themselves, is this mysterious power that enables these people to remain so calm—even joyful—in the middle of terrible circumstances?

Most of our trials are featherweight compared to what the martyrs of old endured. As Scripture reminds us, most of us have never suffered to the point of shedding blood in our struggle against sin (Hebrews 12:4). No lions, no fiery death at the stake, no facing a firing squad.

When we *do* suffer—whether from the bumps and bruises of daily living or for our testimony for Christ—we ought to respond with double the thanksgiving and triple the joy.

The Lord has spared contemporary believers in the Western world from so much pain and suffering. He has been so gracious to us! Perhaps even to the point that when trials do come our way we are "surprised . . . as though something strange were happening" to us (1 Peter 4:12).

But it's as true now as it was hundreds of years ago. *The blood of martyrs is the seed of the Church.* And nothing will convince and convict those around us like the peaceful and positive way you and I respond to our twentieth century hurts and distress. The unbelieving world—your neighbors, the guy at the gas station, the postman, the lady at the cleaners, your boss at work—is observing the way we undergo our trials.

By God's grace, you can hang on without a grumble or complaint . . . remain joyful in tribulation . . . shun the temptation to grandstand as a "martyr" . . . offer thanks in all things . . . trust and obey, no matter what.

It may not be martyrdom, but it will still startle and puzzle a watching world. It will still compel seeking men and women to reconsider Jesus.

RESPONDING TO CIRCUMSTANCES

It's one thing to reflect a submissive attitude toward God when we bring troubles on ourselves, but it's a different matter when unexpected trials smash us broadside—trials not of our own making.

A drunk driver veers across the yellow line. A grim-faced doctor diagnoses some strange cancer. Reassessment slaps your property into a higher tax bracket. Some dumb linebacker breaks your high schooler's leg in football practice. A quick-handed thief lifts your purse or wallet. An old friend drags your name through the mud.

These are circumstances, allowed by God, over which you have no control. And they're the hardest ones to deal with.

But let's look for a moment at the apostle Paul. Talk about getting blindsided with problems over which he had no responsibility! Listen, Paul didn't bring that shipwreck on himself. It wasn't his idea to generate a death threat in Damascus and face the humiliation of leaving town in a basket over the wall. It was never in his mind to orchestrate a mob scene in Lystra, leaving him smashed by stones and left for dead. Was it his choice to enlist a shrill-voiced slave girl to follow him around, causing a ruckus that gave him a bad name? And when he answered people's questions, could he help it if they were outraged by the truth?

No, Paul may not have been responsible for his circumstances. But Paul was responsible for the way he *responded* to those circumstances.

And how did he respond? He didn't groan, "Oh, for Pete's sake, here we go again." Instead, he said, "For Christ's sake, I delight in weaknesses . . . For when I am weak then I am strong" (2 Corinthians 12:10). He said, "Therefore I endure everything for the sake of the elect, that they too may obtain the salvation that is in Christ Jesus, with eternal glory" (2 Timothy 2:10).

Consider the incident in Philippi, described in Acts 16. The magistrates handcuffed Paul and Silas to a scourging pole and gave them a brutal whipping. Piling humiliation upon humiliation, the Philippian authorities then took the bruised and lacerated missionaries and placed them in stocks in an inner cell of the city jail. There they were, stuck in a wet, stinky dungeon tucked far away from the light of day.

Paul must have been faint. Silas must have been sick to his stomach. Every bone ached and their fresh wounds oozed.

Yet, deep in the dark dungeon, they do the incredible. At midnight, the darkest and loneliest hour, they begin praying and singing praises to God. They weren't just humming along lightly or mumbling their prayers in between moans and groans. No, in spite of the thick walls and heavy doors, Luke says that the other prisoners "were listening to them."

Their words won the battle against Satan in that midnight hour. As it says in Psalm 106:47, "Save us, O Lord our God, and gather us . . . that we may give thanks to your holy name *and glory in your praise*." To whine or grumble, fret or murmur, complain or lament, would have been to invite defeat in that terrible hour. And who would have blamed Paul and Silas if they had sputtered a nasty remark or two?

But the record shows they didn't. They didn't succumb in defeat with thoughtless, ill-tempered words. They triumphed in a victory of praise. What a witness to the other prisoners! What a testimony to the jailer! And what an encouragement to countless generations of oppressed believers who have read that account and found fresh courage.

Words. Do we fully understand their power? Can any of us really grasp the mighty force behind the things we say? Do we stop and think before we speak, considering the potency of the phrases we utter?

No wonder the Bible gives so much attention to the phrases which pass through our lips. Little wonder the book of James gives the tongue such a vigorous once-over. How can we bless at one moment and curse at another? How can sweet water and bitter bubble up from the same spring? I shudder to think of all the times during the course of one day that I mutter a complaint or manipulate with a precisely timed phrase or two.

If you and I are looking for victory over our circumstances, we will find it in praise. No matter how much your kids bug you, no matter how often you feel stepped on by others, no matter what the circumstances at home or the office . . . success is possible when we hold our spiteful tongue and win the battle with words that bless our Lord.

We *are* responsible. Maybe we're not accountable for some of our trials, but we are accountable for all of our responses.

If Paul and Silas could sing choruses in a dungeon, you can offer praise wherever life places you. This very moment.

LET YOUR LIFE OVERFLOW

I was reading Psalm 23 the other day and pulled to a dead stop at three familiar words: *"My cup overflows."*

What in the world does that mean?

When something overflows, we usually think of *waste*. Water that overflows a dam rushes out to sea. Gas that overflows a tank pollutes the ground. Coffee that overflows a cup stains the carpet. Milk that overflows a measuring cup drains down the sink. Most folks tend to equate "overflow" with "waste" or "squandered resource."

But what about a *life* that overflows? What about a man or woman who brims over with the joy and grace and love of God? Is it all down the drain? Listen to how Romans 15:13 describes it:

> May the God of hope fill you with all joy and peace as
> you trust in him, so that you may overflow with hope
> by the power of the Holy Spirit.

God must think that sort of overflow is a good idea. He doesn't seem a bit worried about a wasted resource.

Paul might have put his finger on a reason for that in his letter to the Thessalonians:

> May the Lord make your love increase and overflow
> for each other and for everyone else, just as ours does
> for you (1 Thessalonians 3:12).

What a picture! God doesn't intend your life to overflow down the storm drain or evaporate into the air. He wants it to soak others! The spillover of His love and goodness in our lives is to benefit and encourage those around us.

You can't escape it. It's unavoidable. If you want to make an impact for Christ on your family, friends, neighbors, or co-workers, then let God fill you with His joy and peace as you trust Him—just like it says in Romans. He'll fill that cup of yours to the brim, and then pour in more. And over it goes, right over the edges of your soul. Your love will stream out in all directions.

Your joy will cascade like an artesian well, soaking into the thirsty ground of the discouraged and cynical lives around you.

"It was by the generosity of God . . . that the love of God overflowed for the benefit of all men," Paul wrote in Romans. God wants *you* to benefit others, too. So let your cup run over. It's no waste. Nothing will go down the drain or be lost. Trust Him. Obey Him. Then let God open His floodgates in your life, pouring in more of His grace and peace than you could possibly contain.

Listen, you conservative Christians . . . God has never asked any of us to conserve His love.

GRACE SUFFICIENT

The world says, "What can't be cured must be endured."

Christians say, "What can't be cured can be enjoyed."

Do you believe that?

The apostle Paul assures us it is possible when he writes, *"most gladly therefore will I rather glory in my infirmities"* (2 Corinthians 12:9, KJV). His thorn was still sharp, his wounds were still deep.

But he found God's grace to be more than adequate.

Grace. It was available and abundant to me last week when I entered the hospital for minor surgery. Because of my disability, *no* surgery is really minor. My doctors had to take all kinds of weird, complex precautions: special anesthesia, special pre-op preparations, special i.v. hookups, specialized monitoring of my blood pressure and pulse, even extra hours in recovery.

As I was awake for the operation, it didn't occur to me until halfway through that I ought to be panicking. Tubes in and out of me, blood pressure shooting up and down, oxygen mask . . . the works. What did occur to me halfway through was that I was humming a hymn.

Grace, grace, God's grace, grace that will pardon and cleanse within . . .

My Jewish doctors didn't seem to mind the serenade.

This is going to sound crazy, but that was one operation I not only endured, but enjoyed. Why? Because God's grace is not only adequate, it is available for every time of need. We don't have to plead for it, beg for it, or do penance to be worthy of it. No. God's grace—His love in action—is not a favor for which we must implore, it is a gift we are invited to enjoy.

We don't need to ask God to make His grace sufficient for us; He has already assured us that whatever the hardship, there is an equal and compensating amount of grace ready and available for the taking. Grace has been given and it only remains for us to receive it.

How wide and deep and high and long the promise of that grace really is! It *is* sufficient.

So whatever your particular heartache or headache, approach the throne of grace with confidence so that you may find grace to help you in your time of need.

Drink deep of it. It's yours. And it's enough.

SPREADING SUNSHINE

When I was little I loved to pal around with my Uncle Eddie.

He was so much fun. Whenever we'd go camping with my aunt and uncle I'd stick to him like a little shadow. I guess it was because he was always smiling or joking or throwing us kids around—tumbling or wrestling with us.

As long as I can remember, he has hummed, whistled, or sung that old tune,

> You are my sunshine, my only sunshine.
> You make me happy when skies are gray.
> You'll never know, dear, how much I love you.
> Please don't take my sunshine away.

I love that song—and he loved to sing it. Still does, as a matter of fact.

Uncle Eddie has mastered an art I sincerely wish more of us would practice. Simply spreading sunshine. Most people are starved for a smile or a kind word. What a privilege it is when we can give those who are without a reason for smiling our own laughter and joy.

Jesus did much the same thing. Yes, in many ways He was the "man of sorrows." Yet there was something about Him . . . something that *drew* men, women, and children into His company. Peter, an eyewitness to the ministry of the Lord Jesus, tells us, "He went around doing good" (Acts 10:38). Even on the night He was betrayed, He led His men in a hymn of praise.

To the burdened-down men and women He encountered on His journeys, people without smiles, I can well imagine Him giving His own, backing up His command to love one another with a powerful example.

It's sad and ironic that many of us who call ourselves by His name, those of us who possess the very key to life, tend to appoint ourselves as frowning, narrow-eyed judges over the attitudes and actions of others. Somehow we get the idea that *we* are to be the judge, rather than Christ. That it is our responsibility to convict, rather than the Holy Spirit's. We start categorizing other Christians, judging their weaknesses and classifying them as "strong believers" or "backsliders."

We get so picky. So hard. So inflexible. So humorless.

So ungodly.

Yet if we'd only allow the love of Christ to bubble up in our hearts and flow unrestricted through our lives, then we would gladden the strong believer and strengthen the weak one. We'd even be used to draw those outside of Christ into His life-changing embrace.

To state it simply, we would be spreading sunshine. Not the shallow, plastic kind, but the genuine article . . . the Sonlight that brings hope, fresh courage, a reason to live, and—yes!—eternal salvation.

Think of Jesus, who went about doing good, even though the folks around Him were without a smile. Don't get angry at the person who acts in ways that displease you. Give him the smile he lacks. Spread the sunshine of your Lord's limitless love.

In doing so, you just might make your *own* day a little brighter than it was before.

More Than Conquerors

The word seemed to climb off the page. I'd noticed it before, of course. Many times. But why hadn't it ever struck me like this before?

I'd been reading Romans, chapter eight. And in the midst of this familiar portion of Scripture I read again the familiar verse:

No, in all these things we are more than conquerors through him who loved us (v. 37).

More?

What does it mean to be *more* than a conqueror? You'd think it would be enough to conquer in the "things" Paul refers to—things such as trouble, hardship, persecution, famine, nakedness, danger, and the sword (v. 35). What MORE could we possibly do?

I've pondered that. And I may have gained some insight into that verse recently in an unusual place: the middle of a newspaper story. It was an article about a young Christian woman with two artificial legs. About halfway through the story, the reporter captured a surprising statement: "Just as I began to believe that I had conquered this thing called 'disability,'" the young woman said, "I learned that it was not a thing to be conquered. Rather, it was something to accept."

That girl's story got me thinking. The world could expect someone like her to "conquer" the limitations of her severe disability—to defeat, to overthrow, to subdue her problem to the point where she gains mastery over it. To do so would make her an admirable conqueror.

But God expects us to go a giant step further. Through Christ we can do more than merely conquer; we can accept. We can embrace. We can welcome. We can, as the apostle suggests, "consider it pure joy" (James 1:2).

That's exactly what the woman with the artificial legs did. In Christ, she did not simply defeat or "conquer" her difficult circumstances. No. She joyfully accepted each as an opportunity to share in the sustaining, empowering grace which made her *more* than a conqueror.

You needn't have two artificial legs to understand what that young woman was talking about. You could have two artificial humanoids for teenagers. Or twenty-two nagging, insistent demands on your time and energy. Or any number of nettlesome situations you feel need to be conquered in order to be lived with.

To conquer is a human accomplishment, something achieved through willpower, grit, and sheer determination.

To accept goes beyond that. It requires something more than human strength. Something more than a conqueror.

It requires the intrusion of Christ.

LET IT SHINE

This little light of mine, I'm gonna let it shine,
This little light of mine, I'm gonna let it shine,
let it shine, let it shine, let it shine . . .

The familiar little children's chorus has a solid biblical foundation. While He was in the world, the Lord Jesus was the light of the world. Now He's passed that designation along to you and me. "You are the light of the world," He tells us. "A city on a hill cannot be hidden. Neither do people light a lamp and put it under a bowl. Instead they put it on its stand, and it gives light to everyone in the house. In the same way, let your light shine before men" (Matthew 5:14-16).

Quite a responsibility, wouldn't you say?

When God describes His awesome holiness, the analogy again is light. "God is light," John affirms, "in him there is no darkness at all" (1 John 1:5).

When I think of God in that context, I imagine Him as a God who "lives in unapproachable light" (1 Timothy 6:16). Imagine pressing your open eyes against a gigantic searchlight. Who could peer into such a light without going blind?

Yet the Bible goes on to say we are to be holy as He is holy. We are to walk in the light as He is in the light. Somehow, something of the brilliance of God's character is to be displayed through the lives of His sons and daughters on earth.

What kind of light are you?

Me, I'm no searchlight, let alone a supernova. Yet God expects me to shine, shine, shine.

Thankfully, light can be one hundred percent light and still have different *intensities*. Some Christians I know are like candles: they glow with a warmth that draws people to them. Then again, you have the flashlight sort of believers who seem to be able to look right through you. Christians with the gift of teaching remind me of reliable, steady light bulbs—dispelling darkness, showing things for what they truly are. Then there are the laser-types, cutting right through the tomfoolery and getting things done. Searchlight people have a way of leading others out of darkness and guiding and directing them back to safety.

Regrettably, some believers display an inconsistent light. Like matches, they "get on fire for the Lord," but quickly burn out. Others are like skyrockets—a brilliant flash that leaves stunned observers staring . . . but still in the dark.

The bottom line is that God wants us to be His lights in the world. The best lights we can be. With Him as the power source, we're to shine in whatever capacity we can. It may be a bright radiance, a warm glow, a piercing reflection, or a steady beam. Different individuals with diverse personalities, strengths, and weaknesses will display His light with varying intensities. But it's genuine light, all the same, and this darkened world can never have too much.

Let it shine!

OBEDIENCE

*Coming Back
to His Control*

OBEDIENCE
Coming Back
to His Control

Have you ever read a verse scores of times and yet never had it affect you? Then you casually pass by it again and—*zap!*—it hits you squarely between your heart and mind.

There are times when you welcome the Spirit's intrusion. The new insight makes you smile. Out of nowhere you see what God means. A bright new idea opens up.

At other times . . . no smiles. The new insight only brings a groan or tears. You're convicted of manipulating a friend. You're crushed over snubbing a new coworker. Shamed for gossiping about a neighbor. You've been wounded by the Word of God, and you have no excuse not to obey from then on.

Andrew Murray put it this way:

Jesus has no tenderness toward anything that is ultimately going to ruin a man in service to Him. If God
brings to your mind a verse which hurts you, you may
be sure that there is something He wants to hurt.[3]

That's the way God works. He is so very exacting. That's
because He doesn't want us to see our disobedience vaguely or in
general. Specific verses have a way of convicting us specifically.

It happened to me just the other day. I was reading through
the third chapter of John and came across a verse I've glossed
over at least 189 times. But that day, the words of Jesus stung me
like a whip.

Just as Moses lifted up the snake in the desert, so the
Son of Man must be lifted up, that everyone who
believes in him may have eternal life (vv. 14-15).

It all started with an odd question from the Spirit: *Do you
like snakes?*

Snakes? I hate 'em. They're repulsive. Disgusting. Detest-
able. I want to turn away every time I see one. But what does this
verse have to do with snakes?

You tell Me, I sensed the Spirit prodding.

Well, Jesus must have had a reason for using the words
"snake" and "Son of Man" in the same sentence.

So . . .?

So I guess He was likening Himself to the brass serpent
which Moses put on a pole—the serpent which mortally
wounded people gazed upon in order to be saved.

So Jesus made Himself to be a serpent . . . a serpent of sin.

Jesus likened to a snake? Never! Snakes are too disgusting.
Too . . . evil.

*Ah, but Jesus BECAME sin for you. Just how do you think the
Father looked at His Son—His Son who had become sin?*

72

That's when it hit. It suddenly dawned on me why Jesus used a snake to describe His own crucifixion. When the Father turned His back on His Son, He was repulsed over the loathsome object of sin Jesus had become—a despised serpent of sin. Little wonder God turned away from His Son, forsaking Him. Perhaps God felt the same way I do when I want to turn my back on a disgusting, repulsive snake.

Sin *is* loathsome, horribly offensive to God. And when I consider that my sin—individual, particular sins like snide remarks, deliberate exaggerations, prideful actions—drove such a wedge between the Father and His beloved Son on the cross . . . I am heartbroken. Overwhelmed. Humbled.

God wounded me with those verses from John 3. Yet I'm sure there was something He wanted to hurt: my tendency to view disobedience as a vague generality. You see, I'm less likely to correct my disobedience when sin comes plain-wrapped as generic wrongdoing, obscure and ill-defined. I'm more likely, however, to correct my offense when the Spirit pinpoints a particular sin.

Our specific sins hurt Jesus specifically. Understanding what our disobedience did to Jesus, and seeing how our disobedience repulsed the Father, we should want to make certain we keep our lives pure. Doesn't it make your heart break? Overwhelm you? Humble you . . . just a little?

I hate snakes. I only wish I hated my sin half as much.

OLD HABITS DIE HARD

When I was hospitalized as a teenager I met a man hampered by a severe limp. I'd see him every morning, hobbling down the hallway on his lame joints with the aid of a walker. All of us on the floor were looking forward to the day when radical surgery would correct his disability.

That day finally came. The surgeons opened him up and replaced several diseased joints. His lameness was cured.

Yet for nearly a year after that successful surgery, the man continued to limp. I remember greeting him when he came back to the hospital for a visit. There he was, using his cane and walking with a limp.

"That's a shame his surgery didn't take," I commented to a doctor one day.

The surgeon shook his head. "Oh, but it *did* take," he told me. "You see, that man limps out of nothing more than habit."

The dear man had developed strong habit patterns over his years as a disabled person. And even though he was physically free from limping, he still tended to slip back into the old ways.

In a similar manner, we Christians tend to sin . . . mainly out of habit. We *know* that in Christ we have died to sin and its rule over us. Sin no longer has power over us because we have been freed through the death and resurrection of Christ. We are completely free to live a life pleasing to the Lord. Read your emancipation proclamation in passages like Romans 6-8, Galatians 2:20, 1 Peter 2:24, and 2 Peter 1:3-4.

But old habits die hard. For lame men. And yes, for Christians. When we become Christians, we are spiritually free from the grip of sinful thoughts and actions. But unfortunately, as unbelievers we develop strong habit patterns over the years. Often we find ourselves slipping back into old ways—the ways of disobedience and death.

It's habit to look out for ourselves instead of others.

It's habit to retaliate when someone hurts us.

It's habit to indulge our appetites.

It's habit to live for ourselves and not for God.

When we become Christians, it's like having radical surgery—a heart transplant, if you will. Yet it's a struggle to drop all those old habits overnight. In fact, you and I will spend the rest of our lives putting off these filthy old garments, and putting on new habits of holiness.

I like the way Paul put it in Romans 13:14:

> Rather, clothe yourselves with the Lord Jesus Christ, and do not think about how to gratify the desires of the sinful nature.

You know what old, sinful habits you're leaning on today. They die hard, don't they? Whether it's shading the truth, forcing your own opinions on others, a little lustful fantasizing, whatever.

Today, quit leaning on those rotten old crutches. You are *free* from the power of those dark habits, so start acting like it. Join Paul in declaring these bright words of freedom:

> I have been crucified with Christ and I no longer live, but Christ lives in me. The life I live in the body, I live by faith in the Son of God, who loved me and gave himself for me (Galatians 2:20).

Your radical surgery was a complete success.

A Sweet-Smelling Savor

On a cold, crisp day you can catch the scent of a seasoned wood fire from a neighbor's chimney. You can lean out of a back bedroom window, draw a deep breath, and almost taste the scent of pine from the little woods on the other side of the fence.

Speaking of fragrances, I love the smell of fresh, damp laundry hung outside on the line. In the cool air, it smells warm and wet and even a little perfumy from the rinse cycle. As a teenager I would help my mom hang the laundry on the line out back. I used to love burying my nose in my father's damp tee-shirts. They'd smell so fresh.

To this day, catching a whiff of "Tide" laundry detergent brings to mind that wonderful memory of helping Mom. Fragrances have a way of bringing long-ago memories vividly to mind as if I'd encountered them yesterday. I'm sure that's why the perfume industry hauls in mega-millions of dollars. Those guys know how a hint of English Leather or Chanel No. 5 can make us recall warm memories and warm embraces. So crystal clear, so compelling.

For all of that, God's Word spoke of the power of fragrance centuries before Revlon. To the Corinthians, Paul wrote:

> Thanks be to God, who always leads us in triumphal procession in Christ and through us spreads everywhere the fragrance of the knowledge of him. For we are to God the aroma of Christ among those who are being saved and those who are perishing (2 Corinthians 2:14-15).

Paul drew the word picture of the "triumphal procession" from the Roman practice of a military victory parade after a successful campaign. The apostle compares himself first to one of the prisoners led in long chains behind the conqueror's chariot; then to a servant bearing incense; and lastly to the incense itself that wafted all along the parade route.

Paul knew the power behind a sweet fragrance. It was as though he was saying, "I want to live in a way that will perpetually remind God of the obedience, sacrifice, and devotion of the Lord Jesus. I want my words and deeds to bring to the mind of God fragrant memories of the earthly life of Jesus."

Isn't that a startling thought?

Just think of how the smell of a cherrywood fire will bring to your mind rich, deep-rooted memories that bring a smile to your face. In the same way, the Bible is telling you that your life of obedience can actually please God with an aroma that reminds Him of the obedience of Jesus.

So let's not allow disobedience to make our lives a stench. You are called, you are *privileged*, to be a sweet-smelling savor.

Be fragrant. Be obedient. Be God's memory of Jesus . . . a fresh aroma of God's Son through the stale atmosphere of a dying world.

WHERE DISCIPLINE BEGINS

My husband, Ken, a former football coach, links the concept of discipline with a tough, regimented, he-man approach to godly living. He so desires to be a man after God's own heart. Ken longs for discipline.

Just last Sunday our pastor, Dr. John MacArthur, gave an excellent sermon on the subject. I'll tell you, my husband was ready to hear it. With pencil poised over his notepad, he was on the edge of the pew, ready for whatever new insights from God's Word might come his way.

Well, my tough and wonderful man of God got a real surprise.

Instead of hearing a rousing trumpet call spurring him on toward that life of discipline, he heard a truth he wasn't quite prepared for.

"Where do we begin discipline?" Dr. MacArthur began. *"Begin by cleaning your own room!"*

That sat Ken back in the pew. I could almost detect disappointment in his face. I think he would have answered the call if Dr. MacArthur had asked him to jump out of an airplane, fast for two weeks, or climb a mountain in his bare feet.

But clean his room?

We laughed about it on the way home . . . because you should see Ken's fishing room! That's the little room where he keeps his rods and reels, tackle boxes and mounted trophies. Just between you and me—it's been a mess. And he knows it! He also knows that *he must begin there* . . . putting away his tackle box, cleaning up his boots, hanging up his slicker.

For Ken, the discipline must begin with one messy room.

But I think there's a lesson in this for all of us. It's just possible that we—in pursuit of the disciplined life—focus our eyes on larger-than-life goals. We take on three jobs at church. We memorize not only verses, but chapters. We sell the TV or get up at 4:00 A.M. every morning for devotions.

Now, all of these are worthy goals, but it may be that we've overlooked more immediate and obvious things. We've passed over things like a clean room, or being on time, or curbing our tongue. We've neglected for years those "messy rooms" of our lives—those little things that may speak much more eloquently about our discipline than how much we "know."

I took a peek into Ken's fishing room on my way to work this morning. And you know what? It's clean.

My tough, he-man husband who desires to be a man after God's own heart is on his way to really being disciplined.

What's the Cost? Obedience

When Alexander the Great was asked how he conquered the world, he replied, "I acted time after time without delay."

Charles Spurgeon, the great Baptist preacher of England, said, "We often make a mistake when we dilly-dally around when God asks us to do what is a known Christian impression. Why do we waste God's time and our time when what is our Christian duty to do, we ought to do?"

And look at Abraham, the Old Testament patriarch. God said to him, "Leave your country, your people and your father's household and go to the land I will show you." And what was his response?

So Abram left, as the LORD had told him (Genesis 12:4).

Our sense of urgency about doing God's will probably looks small in light of those examples. All too often, when God tells us to get up and do something, we find it difficult to crank our engine. We shuffle our feet and rationalize that we're not quite certain we heard God correctly. We check and double-check the inward call to obey so many times that, before you know it, we've reasoned away the command to obey God. We're certainly not like Isaiah, who heard the voice of the Lord, jumped up and exclaimed, "Here I am, Lord. Send me!"

Are we willing, like Abraham, to exchange the known present for the unknown future?

Are we willing to face the risks of obeying God?

Do we respond immediately?

Maybe we would if we understood that obedience means blessing. God always keeps His Word, and when we live in obedience to that Word, our lives will be blessed. Oh sure, there will be cost—even pain.

God told Paul to go to Macedonia and in obedience he did. And sure enough, it was there in Philippi that Paul was imprisoned.

God told Peter to preach the gospel and in obedience he did. Yet Peter, at the end of his journey, was crucified upside down.

Now, obedience won't always cost us our lives; but it may cost us our comfort, some popularity, position, or prestige. Our friend Abraham gave up his extended family, job, possessions, future security, and even his country.

He said to God, "I will obey." God said, "I will bless you." And He did.

You and I simply don't have time to shuffle our feet and display a "ho-hum" attitude about obeying God. If your get-up-and-go has got up and went where it concerns obedience, then go get it.

That may very well be your first step today toward obeying God's call.

THAT'S GOD'S GLORY ON YOUR FACE

There's something different about the way I look when I'm walking in obedience to God. I don't know how to describe it. Maybe it's a brightness in the eyes. Maybe I find it easier to smile. A kind of glow, maybe?

I don't know quite what it is, but it's there. It's different. It happens when I'm crowding myself close to the Lord and submitting my words and thoughts and actions to Him. It's as though "the glory of the Lord fills His temple."

"Come on, Joni," you tell me, "don't get carried away." Okay. Yet there really is something to it.

In the book of 1 Kings, God told Solomon His glory would fill the temple as long as Solomon and the rest of the people remained loyal to Him.

Did it ever!

> When the priests withdrew from the Holy Place, the cloud filled the temple of the LORD. And the priests could not perform their service because of the cloud, for the glory of the LORD filled his temple (8:10-11).

But in the ninth chapter, God warned that His glory would depart from the temple if the people disobeyed and turned away from Him. He even went so far as to say that everyone—even people outside Israel—would notice that God no longer occupied the temple. The building would still be standing, the priests would still go in and out performing their duties; but the presence of God's fullness would be gone, and everybody would notice the change.

I don't want to push the analogy too hard, but I think there's a sense in which this applies to you and me. Today, we are the temple of the Holy Spirit. He takes up residence in these bodies of ours, and when we obey His commands we are filled to brimming over with His Spirit.

People can't help but notice.

They see a change, however subtle.

On the other hand, when we turn our back on God's Word and plunge headlong into sin, His Spirit no longer fills us. He is quenched. He is grieved. Oh, He still resides within us, but He no longer fills us with His glory. As in Solomon's day, the glory of the Lord departs from His temple.

Am I talking to you today? Are there times when you've pulled a clever disguise over some sin in your life? Perhaps you've tried to hide some secret rebellion from the eyes of others. You've tried to conceal it from your church, from all your Christian friends. You've put on your Sunday best, a fresh shirt and a silk tie. You've put on your makeup, powdered your nose, and painted a nice wide smile on your face. *Nobody will detect it*, you think.

But they will. I'm speaking from experience. They will!

So take this as a friendly caution today. Get right with God and clean out your temple so that the fullness of His glory may return. And return it will, bringing a breath of fresh air and that indescribable glow back to your face.

When God's Spirit is filling you, spilling out all the doors and windows, everybody is going to notice.

THE COUNSEL OF ACHAN

Think of someone you wish you could come alongside to help today.

Take a minute to visualize that person's face. A close Christian friend, perhaps, or a family member living far away. You'd love to reach across the miles with a gift of strength wrapped in the sunlight of encouragement. You'd love to inspire him or her to walk straight paths and stay close to the Lord.

Yes, you can pray. Please do. You can also pick up the phone or drop a card in the mail. But there is something else. Something you might not have considered. Something mysterious and powerful.

It has to do with an obscure little story about a man named Achan.

In Joshua 7 we read about the astonishing victories which Joshua and his citizen army secured for God and His people. But God laid down some strict guidelines about these conquests.

After the battle of Jericho, for instance, God made it clear that all the booty—whether gold or silver, bronze or copper— was to go directly into the Lord's treasury. No one was to line his pockets with Jericho's plunder; these things were to be consecrated to God and kept in His sanctuary.

But Achan had other ideas. He tucked away a few of those costly items for his future retirement and told no one about it except his family. He thought He was getting away with something, but He didn't count on God the Intruder. He didn't consider his all-knowing, all-seeing Lord.

The Lord knew all about it.

Joshua 7:1 tells us that "God's anger burned against *Israel*"—the whole nation! In fact, the very next battle which Joshua led was a disaster. The Israelites were beaten and humiliated by a wimpy, rag-tag militia. And that evening the people stood in disbelief around thirty-six fresh graves. Thirty-six sons and husbands didn't come back to their tents and firesides that night . . . and never would.

Wasn't this the same army that had defeated mighty Jericho? What had gone wrong? Why had the Lord withdrawn His blessing at such a critical moment?

General Joshua was beside himself. He tore his clothes and literally fell on his face in the dirt before the ark of the Lord.

But listen to the Lord's amazing words to His servant:

> Stand up! What are you doing down on your face? Israel has sinned; they have violated my covenant . . . They have taken some of the devoted things; they have stolen, they have lied, they have put them with their own possessions. That is why the Israelites cannot stand against their enemies; they turn their backs and run because they have been made liable to destruction (7:10-12).

Then Joshua got wind of what Achan had done. It was because of this one man's greed and disobedience that God's anger had been kindled against the rest of the people.

You can read for yourself how Joshua and Israel dealt with Achan. But the central truth from this chapter is sobering to say the least: the sin of one person affected the whole camp.

It's a valid lesson even today. We may tuck away little sins out of the sight of others. We might cleverly disguise the way we manipulate other people. We might falsely accuse folks behind their backs. We might chip in our two cents' worth when people are huddled around gossiping. We might hide some private fantasies which dishonor and displease God.

If Achan could speak to us today, he would warn us that our sins will find us out. Our disobedience can—and does—affect the rest of the body of Christ. When we stumble and fall into sin, we're setting the stage for others to do likewise. Like the camp of Israel, God still deals with His Church as a whole, and we mustn't think we can get away with our "little sins" without them affecting our Christian friends.

The book of Ephesians makes it clear we are to care for other Christians because we are one with them. Believers are never told to *become* one—we're *already* one, and we're expected to act like it. Paul first set out that concept in his first letter to the Corinthians. In chapter 12 he says that together, we Christians are like a human body with Christ at the head.

The human body is probably the most amazing example of teamwork anywhere. Every part needs the other. When the stomach is hungry the eyes spot the hamburger, right? The nose smells the onions, the feet run to the snack stand, the hands douse the burger with mustard and shove it back into the mouth where it goes down to the stomach. Now *that's* cooperation!

So we can see why passages like Ephesians 4 tell us that we Christians affect one another spiritually by what we are and do individually.

> Speaking the truth in love, we will in all things grow up into him who is the Head, that is Christ. From him the whole body, joined and held together by every supporting ligament, grows and builds itself up in love, as each part does its work. So I tell you this and insist on it in the Lord, that you must no longer live as the Gentiles do, in the futility of their thinking . . . *for we are all members of one body* (vv. 15-17, 25).

No organ in the body can act without affecting all the rest. The hands that catch the winning touchdown pass bring honor to the whole body—but a sprained big toe can immobilize it.

There is something almost mystical about the intricate, intimate link between us believers.

If we care anything about Christ, the Head of the body, if we care anything about the rest of the body—our wives, husbands, children, or neighbors—we must face our daily challenges and temptations with them in mind.

So what's the "something nice" you can do for your friend today? In a mysterious way, you can help that person in his or her spiritual pilgrimage by simply obeying. Obeying God in all those little tests and struggles this day may bring.

Obedience may seem like a private, personal decision, affecting no one but yourself. That's what Achan thought. And he, being dead, still speaks.

The Mythical Standstill Christian

Open up that great book of imaginary beings and leaf through the listings. Somewhere after Centaur, Goblin, E.T., and Mermaid—but before the Unicorn and the Whatsit—there's a page devoted to an unlikely creature called the Standstill Christian.

It's unlikely because it doesn't exist. There ain't no such thing.

Christians are either growing in the Lord, or going backward. That doesn't leave much room in between. It's like true love: it either grows or it begins to die. Love simply can't stand still, and neither can our walk with Christ.

Little wonder the Bible makes growth such a critical issue. Again and again the writers of the New Testament implore believers to keep moving higher, wider, deeper, and stronger. Listen to a few of them. Can you sense the urgency?

> I keep asking that the God of our Lord Jesus Christ, the glorious Father, may give you the Spirit of wisdom and revelation, so that you may know him better (Ephesians 1:17).

> And this is my prayer: that your love may abound more and more in knowledge and depth of insight (Philippians 1:9).

> One thing I do: Forgetting what is behind and straining toward what is ahead, I press on toward the goal (Philippians 3:13-14).

> This gospel is bearing fruit and growing, just as it has been doing among you since the day you heard it (Colossians 1:6).

> We pray this in order that you may live a life worthy of the Lord . . . bearing fruit in every good work, growing in the knowledge of God (Colossians 1:10).

> May the Lord make your love increase and overflow

for each other and for everyone else (1 Thessalonians 3:12).

You do love all the brothers . . . Yet we urge you, brothers, to do so more and more (1 Thessalonians 4:10).

We ought always to thank God for you . . . because your faith is growing more and more, and the love every one of you has for each other is increasing (2 Thessalonians 1:3).

Fan into flame the gift of God which is in you (2 Timothy 1:6).

Let us leave the elementary teachings about Christ and go on to maturity (Hebrews 6:1).

Like newborn babies, crave pure spiritual milk, so that by it you may grow up in your salvation (1 Peter 2:2).

But grow in the grace and knowledge of our Lord and Savior Jesus Christ (2 Peter 3:18).

It goes on and on. There is simply no room for passivity in the Christian faith. Life in Christ is one long string of action verbs: GROW . . . PRAISE . . . LOVE . . . LEARN . . . STRETCH . . . REACH . . . PUT ON . . . PUT OFF . . . PRESS ON . . . FOLLOW . . . HOLD . . . CLEAVE . . . RUN . . . WEEP . . . PRODUCE . . . STAND . . . FIGHT.

In a child, an animal, a flower, or a tree, lack of growth signals a problem. A healthy life will always show itself by progress and increase. Anything else begins to look like death.

So how can you tell if you're growing? Ask yourself a few simple, direct questions.

Is my sense of sin becoming deeper?

Is my hope brighter?

Is my love more extensive?

Is my spiritual discernment more clear?

Is my faith stronger?

Do I love the Lord Jesus more?

If you can say a hearty "yes" to these questions, then you are on the growing side. If not, then you're doing worse than standing still . . . you are going backwards.

To put it another way, the Christian's transmission is equipped with only two gears: Drive and Reverse. There's no such thing as Neutral—let alone Park.

So wake up! There are grave things at stake here. Look—if your foot had gangrene, you would submit to a severe operation, possibly even amputation, to save your life. Your spiritual state is no less grave.

Don't put yourself in that book of strange, imaginary creatures. If you think you're a Standstill Christian, you're only playing a dangerous game of make-believe.

GOD AND LIGHTNING BOLTS

In a recent article, writer Philip Yancey reflected on a news account of a terrible cathedral fire in England's Yorkminster. The cathedral was destroyed after being struck by a huge bolt of lightning.

Some would say it sounded like an act of divine retribution. The cathedral, you see, was the site of the consecration of an Anglican bishop who had publicly denied both the virgin birth and the resurrection of Jesus Christ.

Now, I can imagine a lot of solid evangelical Christians nodding their heads in agreement. *Served 'em right!*

One problem with the cathedral lightning bolt theory, of course, is that it stands as such an exception. Okay, so fire from the heavens smashes down a liberal, perhaps even apostate church. But what about all the other so-called churches that brazenly deny not only the virgin birth and resurrection, but the majority of other biblical doctrines as well? If God consistently punished bad doctrine with lightning bolts, we wouldn't have any apostate churches—not to mention cult halls, pseudo-Christian temples, and phony religious reading rooms.

No, thankfully, God doesn't normally work that way. There is no relentless reward or punishment system, and I, for one, am glad there's not. Think about it. What if God arranged things so that we would experience a mild jolt of pain with every sin, or a tickle of pleasure with every act of virtue? Sort of a divine behavior modification, if you will. Would you obey because you loved God? I don't think so. I think you'd obey simply because you desired pleasure and not pain.

Yancey puts it like this:

Any covenant requiring consistent reward for our good behavior and consistent punishment for our bad behavior is doomed to fail. We need instead a new covenant with God, one based on forgiveness and grace. And that is precisely why the New Testament exists. It took the most unfair act in history, the execution of Jesus the Christ, to satisfy divine justice in a world full of injustice. That event made it possible for the least deserving of all people—a convicted thief dangling on a cross, for example—to gain an eternity of undeserved happiness.[4]

Ah, but that primal desire for "fairness" dies hard, doesn't it? Who among us doesn't sometimes yearn for a more obvious kind of fairness and justice in this here and now world? We may be tempted to see God's hand behind the headlines of plane crashes, lightning bolts, earthquakes, or AIDS epidemics.

Whenever I'm tempted to think that way, I start reflecting soberly about my own relationship to God. By all that's "fair" I should be on my way to hell. And there was nothing "just" about Christ paying my penalty and the Father adopting me into His family. It was all of His kindness and mercy.

Someday the Judge *will* come to set things right. As John put it, "He will clear his threshing floor, gathering the wheat into the barn and burning up the chaff with unquenchable fire" (Matthew 3:12). Until that time, His method on planet Earth is pure grace.

I wouldn't want it any other way.

God's Part . . . and Ours

I came across a startling statement in a recent study of Genesis 20. In verse 6, God tells Abimelech, *"I have kept you from sinning against me."*

Our logic protests this.

What about the moral responsibility of man? What about our individual freedom? How can God keep us from sinning—and yet insist we are responsible when we do sin?

Good questions.

And that's where grace comes in. I wonder if we really understand the depth and height and power of God's grace? The Bible tells us God's grace is sufficient. It's even sufficient to meet our needs when we're faced with temptation. Don't you think it makes sense, then, that God is really the one who keeps us from sinning when we stand firm and obey?

Ah, but that grace is a gift. Ephesians 2 tells us that. Like any gift, we must take hold of it and make it our own. When we turn down God's gift of grace and choose to follow our sinful nature, doesn't it make sense that such an action is *our* responsibility?

God does His part. He extends His grace—the desire and the power to do His will. What we choose to *do* with His gift is left up to us.

What should be our response to this? We can say, with Paul,

Oh, the depth of the riches of the wisdom
    and knowledge of God!
How unsearchable his judgments,
and his paths beyond tracing out!
. . . For from him and through him
    and to him are all things.
To him be the glory forever! Amen.
(Romans 11:33-36).

God's grace is a gift to be *opened* and *used*.

Are you doing so?

FOCUS

*Looking to Jesus
When Life Gets Confused*

FOCUS

Looking to Jesus
When Life Gets Confused

It's a painting of a
table. But at first glance
you'd never guess.

The legs don't seem
to attach where they
should. The side looks like
the front. The corners almost look inside out. The
top looks upside down. It's
only after you focus on the painting that you begin to
understand.

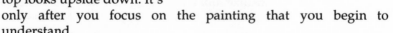

Picasso wanted the viewer to see . . . the impossible.

The painting portrays the table from several points of view.
Shifting your focus, you observe the entire table *at once*—side,
underneath, top, and bottom. What first looks like little more
than some abstract mishmash begins to take shape. The parts of
the table relate. Everything fits together. You're viewing a simple
table—as you've never seen it before.

Extraordinary things can happen with a change of focus. When we think of focus, we usually think of limiting or narrowing our vision. But focus can also mean *expanding* our vision to better understand the entire picture. And when you broaden your vision beyond the obvious, the expected, you're always in for a big surprise.

That's precisely the way we need to focus on the Lord Jesus.

Our ideas about Him are all so neat and tidy and symmetrical. So very right-side-up. Then along comes the Lord and flips our preconceived notions upside-down. In so doing, we begin to see our Master and Savior as we've never seen Him before. We discover that the Lord loves to keep us in perpetual wonder. Focusing on Him that way helps us see . . . the impossible.

I think about that every time I read the story of the two disciples on the road to Emmaus in Luke 24.

They had formed definite ideas about this Messiah around whom they had rearranged their whole life and religious faith. They had always seen Him from one perspective—that of the political savior who would deliver them from the Roman oppressors. Their vision was so narrow and limited that after the Lord's death, nothing made sense. The week's events seemed abstract and confusing—like one of Picasso's wildest paintings. Nothing fit. Nothing related. What else could they do but go home and try to pick up where they had left off before Jesus had come on the scene?

Little did they realize, but a Glorious Intruder was about to enlarge their focus—and give them the surprise of their lives.

As the two disciples walked along the road, lamenting the events surrounding the crucifixion, a Stranger appeared. The Lord Jesus Himself intruded on their conversation, asking them what they were discussing. The disciples, their eyes blinded, may have been annoyed with this uninvited guest. Who was this forward person breaking into their intimate conversation?

But as they traveled, this Man began to broaden their vision. He helped them see things from a different angle as He unfolded the Scriptures and explained how suffering and crucifixion were part of the complete picture.

Their hearts strangely warmed, the two disciples then focused for the first time on this Intruder . . . their risen Lord.

Aaah, so THAT'S what the Scriptures meant. Why, I never saw it that way!

The disciples were beginning to understand things that seemed impossible just moments earlier—all because they looked at Jesus as they had never before looked at Him. And their lives were forever changed.

Wouldn't you like to see a more complete picture of Jesus? One of the most wonderful things about knowing God is that there's always so much more to know, so much more to discover. Just when we least expect it, He intrudes into our neat and tidy notions about who He is and how He works. He delights to turn a situation upside down and show us how the impossible can suddenly become logical.

The Reverend Gregory Hotchkiss writes:

> The Lord does not come to put His stamp of approval upon our views and conclusions about life and about Him and His mission. Rather, He comes and gently, but ever so firmly, intrudes with His Word, and He says, "Listen, it is not as you had thought."[5]

I pray that the next few pages will reveal a perspective of Jesus you have never seen.

THOUGHTS MIDSTREAM

When I was little and went horseback riding with my sisters, I had a hard time keeping up. My problem was that I was riding a little pony only half the size of their mounts. I had to gallop twice as fast just to keep up.

I didn't mind. I took it as a challenge—until we came to the edge of a river. My sisters on their big horses thought it was fun and exciting to cross the river at the deepest part. They never seemed to notice that my little pony sank quite a bit deeper into the swirling waters. It was scary, but I wasn't about to let them know.

One crossing in particular sticks in my memory: the Gorsuch Switch Crossing on the Patapsco River. It had rained earlier that week and the river was brown and swollen. As our horses waded out toward midstream, I became transfixed staring at the swirling waters rushing around the legs of my pony. It made me scared and dizzy. I began to lose my balance in the saddle.

The voice of my sister Jay finally broke through my panic.

"Look up, Joni! Keep looking up!"

Sure enough, as soon as I focused on my sister on the other side, I was able to regain my balance and finish the crossing.

That little story came to mind recently when I was reading about Peter in Matthew 14. It seems he had a similar problem as he walked on the water toward the Lord Jesus. He looked down at the raging waters, got dizzy, and lost his balance. Because he took his eyes off the Lord and put them on the swirling waves around him, he began to sink.

How much we are like him! Instead of resting on the Word of God, we let our circumstances almost transfix us, absorbing us to the point where we begin to lose our spiritual equilibrium. We become dizzy with fear and anxiety. And before you know it, we've lost all balance.

Am I describing you today? Feeling the bite of anxiety? Can't find a babysitter to cover you while you go to that important medical appointment? Can't seem to adjust to life without wheels while your car is getting a new transmission? Are the books just not balancing this month? Maybe your teenager brought over some new friends to the house yesterday—if you could call them friends.

It's easy to panic, isn't it? And admittedly, it's hard to look up—especially when you feel like you're sinking.

But my pony and I made it across the Patapsco and Peter made it back to his boat. Thousands before you, enduring the gale force winds of circumstance, have made it through, keeping their eyes on the Lord Jesus. How about you?

If you can't find a way out, try looking up!

A Lesson from Corrie

A number of years ago Ken and I had the privilege of attending the funeral of Corrie ten Boom. It was a simple service. Brief, not many flowers, very European. But, oh, how challenged we were when we left the church that day.

Several pastors spoke about Corrie's life and work, reading excerpts from her books or recounting incidents from her ministry.

They all talked about her love of Jesus. One pastor said Corrie had specifically instructed him to speak about the love of Jesus—*not* about Corrie ten Boom.

It was the same every time I visited with Corrie or heard her speak. Jesus was always at the center of her thoughts and words. She rarely spoke of "the Christian walk" or "the Christian experience." She didn't speak of Christ as though He were some creed, or doctrine, or lifestyle. She spoke about a Person. A Person she loved more than anyone else in the world.

As Ken and I left the graveside, I remarked that Corrie's life reminded me of Paul's words to the Corinthians:

> When I came to you, brothers, I did not come with eloquence or superior wisdom as I proclaimed to you the testimony about God. For I resolved to know nothing while I was with you except Jesus Christ and him crucified (1 Corinthians 2:1-2).

"How is it," I said to Ken, "that we get so caught up in explaining our walk in Christ, or life in Christ, or some spiritual experience—instead of simply talking about Him?"

I find myself going on and on about my testimony, my trust, my obedience, or "the God of the Bible." I talk more about details and doctrines than I do about Jesus, my Savior and Lord.

I wonder if you find yourself in the same situation. God forbid that we should reduce our Savior to fine-print doctrines squeezed between the pages of a theology textbook. And may the Lord wake us out of spiritual slumber if we catch ourselves making a big deal of our "life in Christ" rather than the simple testimony of Jesus. May we never rely on clever techniques or catchy stories or that manipulative kind of speech Paul spoke of to the Corinthians.

Let's let the life of Corrie speak to us today. So often she would say, "Jesus is Victor!" Let Jesus be our message. Let Jesus be our joy and hope. Let's share who He is today and tell people about our love . . . just for Him.

CRUISING ON GOD'S GRACE

There's nothing like a fancy gadget to make life easier.

That's how I feel about the cruise control switch on my van. As you might imagine, it's not easy for me to keep throwing the weight of my shoulder against the joystick in order to accelerate. So if I'm on a long drive down the freeway, I'll just flick on cruise control and float along at an easy fifty-five miles per hour.

It almost feels like the van is driving itself. It gives itself gas going up hill and levels off on a straightaway. All I have to do is sit in the driver's seat and think about steering. Everything automatic. Everything self-operating. And all so easy.

I suppose the danger is that a driver could tend to depend too much on cruise control, switching his mind off as he sails along that lazy, asphalt river.

I've discovered another kind of cruise control that's even more dangerous. You and I employ it more frequently than we realize.

It has to do with God's grace and the automatic, self-operating view we tend to have of it. Let me describe it for you.

You flop in bed and mumble a good night prayer to God. You wake up in the morning a little later than you should, throw back the covers and hop in the shower, barely giving God or His grace a thought. In the back of your mind you feel like the morning is driving itself, without you deciding much about it. In your least consistent moments, you might even feel as though your whole life is on cruise control. All you have to do is decide which way to steer yourself.

Why do we act like this? Perhaps it's because life seems easier when we assume the grace of God in our lives is as automatic as breathing, as self-operating as the beat of our heart. But it's not that way. When it comes to God's grace, cruise control simply doesn't apply.

God won't let us get away with that sort of sloppy attitude. In 2 Peter 1:2, we're told that grace is ours in abundance *through the knowledge of God and of Jesus our Lord*. In other words, grace comes in abundance only as we get to know Jesus. It only comes as we seek Him in prayer, meet Him in His Word, follow Him through obedience, greet Him in the morning, relax with Him at night.

As in any relationship, it takes work to develop a relationship like that. There's nothing automatic about it.

The old King James Bible puts it nicely: "Grace and peace be multiplied unto you through the knowledge of God, and of Jesus our Lord. . . ."

I like that word "multiplied." I never made fantastic grades in math, but I do know what it means to increase quantity through multiplication. If Peter intended to be mathematical in his word choice, then grace and peace is only increased in our lives as it is multiplied by our knowledge of Jesus.

So let's switch off the cruise control, friends. Life—at least, life in abundance—doesn't work that way.

The grace of God demands our full attention.

A MATTER OF FOCUS

Some of the best counsel I've received in a long time came in a recent letter from a man I've never met.

"Many believers gaze at their problems and glance at the Lord," wrote Ted Smith. "But how much better to gaze at the Lord—and only glance at your problems."

Uncommon good advice, Mr. Smith. Too many of us rivet our eyes on our predicaments. We start measuring the mass of our responsibilities, charting the depth of our dilemmas, adding up the weight of our worries. In so doing, we only give our Lord an occasional worried glance—just to make sure He's still in the vicinity.

It's all a matter of focus, isn't it? Our problems are too real and tangible. The dog tracks Alpo all over the kitchen floor. Your husband calls to say he'll be late (again). The casserole turns to charcoal in your oven and a shouting match erupts between your teenagers upstairs. Little wonder you stand there with your dish towel in hand, droop-shouldered, dumbfounded as to what to do. You mutter an obligatory prayer to God as you tromp up the stairs to referee.

Sound familiar? You've been in plenty of situations like that. Your problems scream for undivided attention; and God barely gets noticed in all the scramble.

How we need to consider again the counsel from Hebrews:

> Let us fix our eyes on Jesus, the author and perfecter of our faith, who for the joy set before him endured the cross, scorning its shame, and sat down at the right hand of the throne of God. Consider him who endured such opposition from sinful men, so that you will not grow weary and lose heart (12:2-3).

That's it, right there. *Consider Jesus.* He had one heavy-duty cross to bear, but He fixed His sight up ahead—on the joy set before Him. And we, as the command makes clear, are to do much the same. Let us fix our eyes on the Author and Perfecter of our faith. That's the focus.

So what's changed about the charred casserole, the dirty kitchen floor, and the argument upstairs? Nothing. But what *can* change? Your focus. Don't lock your gaze onto your problems while you only glance at the Lord. Get it in focus. Gaze at the Lord—behold Him—and your problems won't cause you to grow weary and lose heart.

Try it sometime. Like right now. Write out Hebrews 12:2-3 and tape it above your kitchen sink, to your computer terminal, or to the dashboard of your car. That way, it will always stay in focus.

And so will you.

The Weaker We Feel, the Harder We Lean

I love quoting people who help my walk with the Lord—especially managing life in this wheelchair. Dr. J. I. Packer is a favorite. And believe me, as I quote him, I could make these words my own.

> God uses chronic pain and weakness, along with other afflictions, as his chisel for sculpting our lives. Felt weakness deepens dependence on Christ for strength each day. The weaker we feel, the harder we lean. And the harder we lean, the stronger we grow spiritually, even while our bodies waste away. To live with your "thorn" uncomplainingly—that is, sweet, patient, and free in heart to love and help others, even though every day you feel weak—is *true* sanctification. It is true healing for the spirit. It is a supreme victory of grace. The healing of your sinful person thus goes forward, even though the healing of your mortal body does not. And the healing of persons is the name of the game so far as God is concerned.[6]

The weaker we feel, the harder we lean on God. And the harder we lean, the stronger we grow. You couldn't really describe that as "extraordinary stamina," as some would say of those who suffer. Nor is it "a testimony to human courage," as those same people would say.

Extraordinary stamina and human courage have nothing to do with it. It is human *weakness* God delights in using.

You might have a tough time living with your weakness today. You find it nearly impossible to be "sweet and patient and free in heart to love and help others."

It isn't nearly impossible, it IS impossible. You simply can't manage it while you're trying to find within yourself the stamina or courage to do so. You will fail every time.

Rather, felt weakness should deepen our dependence upon Christ for strength. Remember, the weaker you feel, the harder you must lean. Lean on Jesus. And leaning means trusting, obeying, spending concentrated time talking to Him and sharing your deepest needs.

When you lean that hard, you'll find yourself growing stronger than you ever dreamed possible. As Dr. Packer puts it, that's what true healing is all about.

REFLECTIONS IN A NURSERY

A friend of mine had a baby recently. As I visited the couple's home, I had to admire their elaborate nursery.

They really did it up right! Big Bird nested in the corner, Snuffulupagus perched on the crib side table, and an assortment of Wabbling Weebols, Smurfs, and My Little Ponies encircled the interior of the crib. Not to mention five teddy bears. And a busy box gizmo with umpteen handles, knobs, and twirly things. And two musical mobiles. And who knows how many rattles.

This baby was decked out. There was no way this kid was going to get bored or cranky, right?

Well, not exactly. True, the child will be able to amuse himself, what with so many gaudy toys and wild, wonderful distractions. He should find himself positively absorbed at times by the ministrations of the musical mobiles.

But amusement of that sort only lasts for so long. A child is easily quieted *so long as he isn't hungry.*

But watch out! Once that baby feels the cravings of nature within, absolutely nothing will satisfy but *food!*

So it is with our soul. Distractions and amusements may appease us for awhile—church music, candles, processions, banners, committees, and Christian talk shows. But all these, like gaudy toys, will occupy and entertain for only so long. Sooner or later boredom and frustration set in. Once a believer's conscience is awakened, all of those religious trappings and incidentals simply won't satisfy. Like the writer said in Hebrews 5, you begin to want solid food.

A man or woman animated by the Spirit just *has* to be fed. The cravings of our new nature force us back to the basics—and there begins the glorious pursuit of God. A real Christian will not rest contented with mere appearances. They'll seem like a waste of time.

Are you gathering more spiritual things around you and enjoying it less? Are you bored? Restless? Do you refuse to be entertained? Want something more?

It may be that you're hungry! The cravings of your new nature are giving you hunger pains. And you will not be satisfied until you have real food. Like Jesus says in John 6:35, "I am the bread of life. He who comes to me will never go hungry."

Want to quiet those cravings? Forget the gizmos and doo-dads in the nursery. The King waits at the dining table.

BETWEEN TWO CROSSES

In my weaker moments, I've wondered if the Lord's disciples had as tough a time believing as we do.

After all, they had the benefit of rubbing shoulders with the Master every day for almost three years. As John wrote, Christianity for them was something "which we have heard, which we have seen with our eyes, which we have looked at and our hands have touched" (1 John 1:1).

They were eyewitnesses to the Lord's greatest miracles. They saw dead men raised with a word, lepers healed with a touch, paralytics leap to their feet at His bidding. They watched His hands form fresh bread and charcoal-broiled fish out of thin air—enough to feed thousands of hungry people. They witnessed a boiling sea and a screaming wind fall silent and calm in an instant at His three-word command.

When it comes to the issue of faith, I have to admit, the disciples aren't the ones I identify with most. But there *is* somebody in Scripture who believed in a most extraordinary way.

> One of the criminals who hung there hurled insults at [Jesus]: "Aren't you the Christ? Save yourself and us!"
>
> But the other criminal rebuked him. "Don't you fear God," he said, "since you are under the same sentence? We are punished justly, for we are getting what our deeds deserve. But this man has done nothing wrong."
>
> Then he said, "Jesus, remember me when you come into your kingdom."
>
> Jesus answered him, "I tell you the truth, today you will be with me in paradise" (Luke 23:39-43).

Yes, it was marvelous for the disciples to believe in Jesus. With the exception of the betrayer, those men stuck with the Lord through golden days of glory and storm-darkened days of anxiety and gloom. They had left everything to follow the Lord—even at the risk of their very lives.

But to me, it was an even greater display of faith for this dying felon to put his trust in the Lord. That man on the adjacent cross never had the benefit of seeing all the mighty signs and miracles which flabbergasted the disciples. He never shared in their quiet talks around the evening campfires. He never enjoyed their camaraderie under full sail in an open boat under a wide Galilean sky.

The criminal saw only Jesus in agony, in suffering, and in weakness. He saw Him deserted, mocked, naked, humiliated, and despised. He witnessed no majesty and power—*and yet he believed*.

But whatever this story says about the faith of a penitent thief, it says even more about the One who responded.

> The Lord Jesus never gave so complete a proof of His power and will to save as He did upon that occasion. In the day when He seemed most weak, He showed that He was a strong deliverer. In the hour when the Lord's body was racked with pain, He showed that He could feel tenderly for others. At the time when He Himself was dying, He conferred on a wicked criminal eternal life.[7]

If there was ever a time when Jesus deserved to think a little about His own comfort, it was on the cross. But even there, His thoughts were of others. He offered them hope; He offered them life.

He was reaching out to redeem.

The encounter between those two crosses on that dark day is a story of unceasing wonder. That the same dying Savior would reach down the centuries to save you and me is more wonderful still.

WHEN YOU'RE WEARY

Every once in awhile I daydream back to the days when I was a young child with sturdy, active legs beneath me.

There were so many memorable times with our extended family and friends: camping trips at the beach, picnics along the river, backpack adventures in the mountains.

I remember one particularly long hike with my dad and his friends when I was barely six years old. I scrambled to keep up with the adults, but my little legs—healthy as they were—could only carry me for so long.

I was so weary. So burdened. I remember how thankful I was that my dad and his companions were such big, strong, grown-ups. They would have no trouble carrying a little tyke like me on their broad shoulders.

When my dad finally reached down and slung me on his back, I breathed a huge sigh of relief. I wouldn't have to worry . . . he was strong enough to carry us both.

That memory calls a much-loved Scripture to mind:

> Come to me, all you who are weary and burdened, and I will give you rest. Take my yoke upon you and learn from me, for I am gentle and humble in heart, and you will find rest for your souls. For my yoke is easy and my burden is light (Matthew 11:28-30).

Does anything in that statement strike you as . . . odd?

It seems strange that we don't hear Jesus saying, "Look at Me. Look how big and strong I am. Look how powerful and robust. Notice how dominant. I'm hardy enough to take on your load. Lean on Me because I'm so strong."

No, instead we hear Him saying "Come to me . . . *for I am gentle* and humble in heart."

That's certainly not the message we hear from the world around us. It's the strong, the unwavering, the assertive—those who never shed a tear or admit a weakness—who are portrayed as the competent, capable load-bearers.

The Bible says differently. God's Word reminds us that humility, gentleness, patience, kindness, and goodness tower head and shoulders above the proud, macho stuff. It is the humble and the gentle to whom we find ourselves drawn when we feel burdened or weary. Somehow we know these are the folks who genuinely care, who actually pray. These are the ones willing to come alongside and help shoulder our load.

That's why the words of Jesus are so compelling. He *is* strong . . . but He's also approachable. He *is* able to carry our load . . . but He'll never make us feel embarrassed or defeated for asking.

Are you weary? Weighed down? Exhausted from the journey?

"Cast all your anxiety upon him, because he cares for you."

A fisherman named Peter penned that simple prescription for anxiety and exhaustion almost twenty centuries ago.

No one has improved on it since.

A TWO-FOLD DEFENSE

What's your first response when you're hit with temptation?

The temptation to back away from your testimony . . . to fudge the truth . . . to spread a bit of gossip . . . to dwell on an impure mental image?

In our daily warfare with sin, it is our Enemy's *first approach* that can be the most dangerous. Bolt the door firmly against his first knock, and it will be easier to keep it closed when he begins pounding and kicking later on.

At the beginning of His ministry, our Example showed us a powerful way to thwart temptation's first approach. Satan chose his time carefully. After almost six weeks of fasting in the wild wastes of the Sinai, Jesus must have been faint with hunger.

At that moment of profound human weakness, the devil came calling.

> The tempter came to him and said, "If you are the Son of God, tell these stones to become bread."
>
> Jesus answered, "It is written: 'Man does not live on bread alone, but on every word that comes from the mouth of God'" (Matthew 4:3-4).

Jesus countered attack after attack by quoting Scripture after Scripture, foiling each satanic strike. In so doing, He sketched a wonderful pattern for us.

But Scripture isn't the only defensive weapon in our God-given arsenal. Consider another example Jesus laid down—not at the beginning of His ministry, but at the end.

In the Garden of Gethsemane, the marshaled forces of hell tore at our Lord's humanity, trying to keep Him from the cross. If we could have somehow observed that scene, it would have been a terrifying moment. Had Jesus turned away from Calvary, you and I would be lost for eternity.

Just as the devil had enticed Jesus three times in the wilderness, so He was tempted three times in the garden.

But what does Jesus do this time? *He prays.* And although His friends—His disciples—didn't even stay awake to encourage Him, He continued to pour out His soul. Groaning. Sweating. Agonizing. Lying face down.

At the dawn of His ministry Jesus showed us the importance of using Scripture to fight our Enemy. At sunset, He underscored the use of prayer.

Scripture and prayer . . . those are the weapons. Well do we know that we should use both. But, how hard it is in the middle of our problems to remember these examples of Christ!

Jesus understands even that.

For when He was tempted in the garden, the Son of Man spoke such human words: "The spirit is willing, but the flesh is weak" (Matthew 26:41, NASB). Jesus knew how strong the pull of temptation could be.

Are you weak today, even though your spirit is willing? Are you tempted to open the door "just for a moment" to that persistent knocking?

Whatever the assault may be, it can be overcome. Jesus showed us how, both at the beginning and at the end of His ministry on earth.

Just another reminder that He's with us from start to finish.

TRUST

*Relying On God's Control
When Things Fall Apart*

TRUST
Relying On God's Control
When Things Fall Apart

I know my husband Ken almost—but not quite—like the back of my hand.

I'm not bragging, but honestly, there's hardly a feeling he can hide from me. I know that when his eyes narrow more than usual, he's worried. When his mouth stretches and his lips flatten in a certain funny way, he's irritated. When he spends too much time leafing through fishing magazines, he's depressed.

I also know there's not much Ken likes to keep hidden from me. He's the kind of guy who desires to be transparent, who invites me to know him on a deeper, more intimate level.

And because I know Ken very well, I trust him. In fact, it's almost in mathematical proportion: The more I get to know my husband, the greater my trust in him.

When it comes to our relationship with God, this knowledge-trust formula is more than a matter of mathematics. It's a truth straight out of Scripture. King David put it this way:

> Those who know your name will trust in you,
>   for you, LORD, have never forsaken
>   those who seek you (Psalm 9:10).

It's cause and effect. A direct link. You can't have one without the other. To know God is to trust Him.

That should be good news if you've been troubled lately by a lack of trust, an inability to depend on the Lord through big or little problems. There *is* an answer. If you want to increase your resolve to trust God, to rely on Him faithfully, to depend on Him consistently . . . then you must seek to know Him better.

Paul the apostle understood that. He put Psalm 9 into his own words when he wrote: "I *know* whom I have believed, and am convinced that he is able to guard what I have *entrusted* to him . . ." (2 Timothy 1:12). As far as Paul was concerned, he could unquestioningly trust God with his health, his income, his ministry, and his relationships, simply because he had grown intimate with the Lord.

So how can you get to know God better?

Seek. Look. Search. And be encouraged! Scripture declares that if you "seek the LORD your God, you will find him if you look for him with all your heart and with all your soul" (Deuteronomy 4:29).

That verse gives me the impression God is calling us to spend time with Him beyond what we ordinarily plan. Extra moments outside of our usual Bible study or quiet time.

Ah, but I can almost read your thoughts. *Come on, Joni, be real! I have my quiet time each day, attend Bible study, Sunday school, and church, have nightly devotions with my spouse . . . and now I'm supposed to make MORE time?*

Wait. It's not so much that we "make more time" for Him. It's more a matter of recognizing that *all* of our time is His.

Imagine, for instance, that you're slumped on the couch watching a silly sitcom on TV. During a commercial, the Spirit intrudes, whispering, "Turn it off and spend a few moments with Me."

What's your response?

Or let's say you're tossing and turning in bed, fretful that you can't get to sleep. Out of nowhere the Spirit interrupts your anxiety with a quiet suggestion: "Why don't you use this time to pray?"

Do you?

Or maybe you have a choice between a magazine and your favorite devotional book. The Spirit intervenes, suggesting, "Let's spend time together in that devotional you haven't picked up in awhile."

Which will it be?

God loves to break beyond the bounds of the structured minutes we've scheduled for Him, reminding us that every moment of ours . . . is *His*. Trust can only increase when we redeem those precious, inopportune, untimely moments as ways to know Him better.

That's something to consider as you spend time with the Lord over these next few pages. Each thought, each Scripture is a way of getting to know Jesus a little better . . . and trusting Him a little more.

The moments you invest in this chapter may better prepare you for the next time the Spirit of Christ "trespasses" into those extra moments, inviting you to know Him on a deeper, more intimate level.

BACKED INTO CORNERS

Jesus had a way of exasperating people.

He still does. It only takes a glance through one of the Gospels. Before you know it, you find yourself squirming.

The way Jesus does things—the demands He makes, the example He offers, the way He deals with the status quo in people's hearts—all of it backs you into an uncomfortable corner. What He says about sacrifice, favoritism, bigotry, stewardship, and giving presses your back hard against the bricks. Suddenly, unexpectedly, He's got you thinking—thinking about things you never would have troubled yourself with before you picked up His Word.

In short, you're irritated.

The demands of Jesus always seem to bring crisis into people's lives. He commanded Peter to lower his net, even though He knew Peter had been fishing all night with nary a mackerel to show for it.

He told the rich young ruler to sell all his possessions.

He insisted John baptize Him when doing so would violate John's understanding of Messiah.

He demanded that the religious lawyer—who was far more interested in debate and discussion—*do* what he understood rather than simply talking about it.

Uncomfortable corners. Pinned against a spiritual wall.

But the thing I love most about the Lord Jesus is that He won't allow us to stay pinned against the wall. He doesn't want us to remain in our corners. Ah, but the only way He permits us to peel ourselves off those spiritual walls—the only way He allows us to tiptoe out of those uncomfortable corners—is to follow Him.

Jesus will not liberate us from the quandary He's put us in except to have us follow Him and His example. Jesus doesn't assume you will follow Him—it's too precious a thing to leave to us alone. No, He *commands* that you follow Him.

Is He asking something uncomfortable of you today? To clean up a bad habit? To back off your prejudices? To eat some of your pride? To reach deep in your pocket and give to a person in need? To make amends with an irritating friend?

Welcome to the corner! You're in wonderful company!

Everyone clashes with the Lord Jesus sooner or later, whether they love Him or hate Him. He exasperates. He engineers crises. He compels. He forces you to make a choice.

Wait long enough in that corner and you'll meet. But I'm not staying. I'm going to follow Him out.

WHAT CAN YOU BEAR?

Over the years many people have asked me, "How do you do it, Joni? How do you cope with your paralysis? How can you bear it?"

I've wondered the same thing of others. Every time I look at someone who is totally blind or deaf, I think, *How in the world can they do it?*

I look at my friend, Vicky, who is even more paralyzed than I. I can at least flail my arms and drive a van; she can only shrug her shoulders. Occasionally, I've ventured to tell her, "Vicky, I just don't know how you do it. I don't think I could stand being that paralyzed." But then she looks at people who endure constant pain—and can't imagine what it would be like to live with *that* kind of suffering.

Suffering, and our ability to stand up strong in it, is relative. In 1 Corinthians 10:13, Paul assures us that our Lord will never tempt or test us beyond what we can bear. The apostle further reminds us that God's grace will never be in short supply.

> And God is able to make all grace abound to you, so that in all things at all times, having all that you need, you will abound in every good work (2 Corinthians 9:8).

Through God's grace, Vicky and others like her have been able to bear up under a severe paralysis. But God has not chosen that level of limitation for me. Yes, I am paralyzed, but only to the degree that I can, with His grace, live a joyful and meaningful life.

Not everyone can be trusted with suffering. Not everyone can endure a fiery ordeal. So the Master scrutinizes the jewels and carefully selects those which can bear the refining, the branches which can stand the knife. It is given for some to preach, for others to work, for others to give, and for still others to suffer.

Where do you fit on that scale? Perhaps you're not paralyzed. You may not be deaf or blind or carry the seeds of cancer in your body. God knows that you are not the one to handle— even with all of His resources of grace—that kind of suffering.

But He *has* selected you to handle that particular, unique, individual set of circumstances in your own life. Your singleness. Your marriage. Your sterility. Your prison term. Your finances. Your job. Your unemployment. Your background. Your physical appearance, abilities, and educational opportunities.

Whatever you would call "suffering" in your own life, God has allowed it. Even purposed it.

Don't you dare think you can't handle it! First Corinthians 10:13 promises that you can not only handle it, but glorify God in it.

So don't be looking at the man with cerebral palsy, thinking, *How does he manage?* Don't be looking at the saintly wife who exhibits a submissive and quiet heart in an abusive family situation and think, *I could never do that.* Don't shake your head when you see a mom or dad with a Downs Syndrome child and say, *No way could I face that.*

Most likely you couldn't. Which is precisely why God hasn't asked you to. Instead, take time to seriously consider how you will remain joyful and obedient within your own particular, unique, individual situation. Accept your circumstances as a gift from His hand. Dare to thank Him for them.

Not everyone could be trusted with what you're wrestling with today, but you have been so trusted. Find meaning and joy as you draw on His resources . . . and *persevere.*

The grace is God's. The choice is yours.

LEAD ME TO THE ROCK

When life rushes by too fast, when deadlines pile up and commitments mount by the hour . . . I begin longing for the Sierras.

The world seems a little less crazy after a couple of days on top of a mountain. Those high country panoramas have a way of clearing my head and giving me a fresh perspective. The world and its problems seem a little less overwhelming. Pressures seem somehow less pressing. Life begins to look manageable again.

That's why Psalm 61 remains a real favorite for me. I love it when David says, "From the ends of the earth I call to you, I call as my heart grows faint; lead me to the rock that is higher than I. For you have been my refuge, a strong tower against the foe" (vv. 2-3).

God is the rock higher than you and I. And when our world presses in on us, when deadlines circle like vultures, when commitments cut into our shoulders like a ninety-pound pack, we need renewed perspective. We need a vantage point.

Spending time with God, in the high places of His power and love, we can gain a better, wider view on our lives. He is the mountain towering over our smoggy horizons. Life viewed from His heights can clear our minds, help us sort through priorities, and allow us to see how our days can be managed after all.

Maybe, like me, you've had one whirlwind of a month. You face demands from your family, frustrations at work, commitments at church, and expectations from friends. You feel your heart growing fainter with each added pressure.

You may not be able to take time off and head for the mountains (especially if you live in Kansas). But you can still climb that Rock so much higher than you.

Investing solid, concentrated time with your understanding Lord will give you a whole new outlook. From the summit of His love, you'll see things as they really are.

GOD UP AHEAD

Ever get the feeling you're somewhere out in front of God as you move through your week?

You bump up against a rugged trial or painful heartache, and you know from Scripture that God's going to "work all things together for good"—but somehow you have the idea He's *behind* you, armed with dustpan and broom, ready to do a cleanup job on you and your problem.

Perhaps you imagine Him with a bottle of glue, standing a few paces back, ready to pick up the broken pieces of your life and put it back together again. Or you picture Him with hammer and nails, ready to follow after you and patch things up.

Ever feel that way? As though God's principle activity in your life is to come along behind and throw you a rope after you've fallen headlong into an unexpected pit?

Our imaginations may conjure up that image of God, but it's certainly not a biblical picture. God's Word tells us over and over that the Lord goes *before* us, not just behind.

In Psalm 23 we're reminded He leads us. In Psalm 25 we're told He guides us. Psalm 139:3 (TLB) says, "You chart the path ahead of me, and tell me where to stop and rest." In John 10, Jesus assures us the Shepherd goes "on ahead of his sheep."

So God isn't surprised by your trials. He doesn't push you out ahead, backing you up with a mop bucket and a box of Band-Aids. And He's certainly not caught off guard when your path is filled with pain.

No, He *leads* us, stepping out ahead and blazing a straight path. You can be sure that if He's gone ahead, He has planned every event so that it fits miraculously into a pattern for good in your life. He'll give you the power, grace, strength, and endurance to meet every challenge.

Even today . . . when you're feeling like you're out there all alone.

Even today . . . as the big window pane of your circumstances cracks and shatters into a thousand jagged shards.

God is more than an emergency phone number. He's more than a clean-up crew with hammer and nails and glue. He's more than an insurance adjuster with a sharp pencil and a big checkbook.

He's out in front of you . . . preparing, planning, going before, leading and guiding you every step of the way.

UNNECESSARY GUILT

It's clear God forgives, but have you ever had trouble forgiving *yourself*?

Have you ever been pestered by guilty feelings? You confess and yet feel no relief? Guilt—nagging and constant—can be like trying to balance a heavy boulder on your shoulder.

Frankly, some people who feel the worst condemnation are those with the least reason to feel guilty. I'm speaking here of *needless* guilt.

Let me explain. When I was first injured, lying paralyzed in that hospital bed, my mother suffered unbelievably. She was hounded by guilt over my accident—understandable feelings, but unnecessary.

Mom kept punishing herself for things like not teaching me how to be more cautious around shallow water, not warning me enough about diving where I couldn't see bottom, not enrolling me in a water safety course.

Now, I knew very well my mother wasn't at fault for my stupid dive. If anybody should have felt guilty, it was me. But looking back, I think my mother believed she *had* to punish herself. It was her way of participating in my pain. Her guilty feelings somehow assured her of a share in my burden.

In short, her guilt was a way of identifying.

But that kind of guilt is needless—and a terrible waste of precious emotional resources. All of those "if onlys" act like a powerful corrosive, eating away at the fabric of the soul.

"If only I had stopped my daughter from driving in that car of reckless kids . . ."

"If only my genetics were different, my son wouldn't have been born this way . . ."

"If only I hadn't permitted my boy to sign up for football, he'd be okay and not in that hospital . . ."

"If only I'd been more sensitive to my husband's needs, he wouldn't have left me . . ."

It's so hard to look at hurt and pain in your family and not be tempted to take it out on yourself. It seems almost impossible to say, "What's done is done and I have to go on from here."

Even the apostle Paul had to do that. In Philippians 3:13-14 he puts it this way: "Forgetting what is behind and straining toward what is ahead, I press on . . ."

You might be hurting right now, struggling with the tangled ropes of unnecessary guilt. For the sake of Christ's kingdom—and especially those who need your unhindered, un-diluted emotional energies—please saturate your mind with the promise in Romans 8:1:

> Therefore, there is now no condemnation for those
> who are in Christ Jesus.

God doesn't condemn you for happenings out of your control. And even if those events *were* within your control, His blood can cleanse any sin and launder your heart whiter than new-fallen snow.

Remember, God is the One who wants to help you take the boulder off your shoulder.

God and the "Little Things"

People often ask me, "Joni, how does the devil get to you? What kind of fiery darts really get under your skin?"

I'm not sure if folks expect a laundry list of vices and temptations, but what I tell them most often is this: Satan digs at me hardest when things break down.

My comfort and independence rest heavily on bits and pieces of adaptive equipment. When that equipment fails—a buckle on a corset snap or a clamp on a leg bag or a tire on a wheelchair—well, it really gets to me.

I was explaining that to a friend not long ago.

We wrapped up our conversation as I wheeled into my van. I cranked the engine and was just about to push the control to close the electric-powered door, when my friend reached over, grabbed the handle, and slammed the door shut.

A friendly gesture. One that anybody might do as you're saying goodbye. My car door, however, is loaded with fragile chains and springs and switches. With one good yank from my "helpful" friend—and before I could cry "Stop!"—the door chain snapped.

He was thoroughly embarrassed and I was almost irritated. But we both laughed over our reactions.

You probably feel the same way when your washing machine gets rusty joints, when the printer on your computer freezes up, or your car's air conditioner takes a vacation. Take heart! If God can make axheads float as He did in 2 Kings 6, or if He can cause the wheels to fall off Egyptian chariots as He did in Exodus 15, then God must be in control of the springs and hinges and widgets and all the rest of those little mechanical doodads that seem to break down at the wrong time.

The Bible makes it clear God's control extends beyond the "big things" of life, like our dreams and destiny. We all know the Lord has His hand in those monumental decisions of our lives. But Scripture also tells us the Lord gets down into the nuts and bolts of little things.

I'm trying hard to remember that whenever my wheelchair batteries konk out on me, leaving me stranded where I don't want to be. I'm trying to remember to have a good attitude about those kinds of things, to remember that God is still in control.

The next time you have to call a plumber or have a mechanic look under your hood, remember that the King's sovereignty extends to such lowly, utilitarian objects like refrigerators, toasters, transistors, and oil filters. Even in these, He is Lord.

So hang in there. Be patient. Call a handyman. Pay the bill.

But trust God.

HE CARES FOR YOU

"Cast all your anxiety on him because he cares for you" (1 Peter 5:7).

That's not only a fragment of Scripture, it's a foundation of Scripture.

God's acts of compassion and mercy never go unnoticed by the authors of the Bible. Time and again, God demonstrates His love through this intimate, very personal care of His children.

Some carry this idea even further. God cares so much for us, these individuals say, that He would never want *any* hurt or heartache to touch our lives.

"Why," they reason, "if we really trusted in Him, God would go to any length to release us from our pain."

While no one is saying God enjoys watching our struggles, Scripture clearly indicates that He allows certain wounds and hardships to prick and pierce our lives. But it never means He no longer cares.

God certainly cared for Timothy, who struggled with frequent illness.

He cared for James, run through with Herod's sword because of his testimony.

He cared for James' brother, John, exiled and isolated on a lonely island.

God's care for all these people was not inconsistent with the fact of their suffering. Hebrews 12:5 tells us "the Lord disciplines those he loves."

As Paul sat in a Jerusalem prison cell, the Lord kindly appeared to him and said, "Take courage! As you have testified about me in Jerusalem, so you must also testify in Rome" (Acts 23:11).

God cared about Paul. And no doubt Paul took his friend Peter's advice and cast all his anxiety on God. Yet he remained in custody for at least *two years* after the Lord appeared to him.

Did God stop caring in those two years? Of course not. God answered His servant's prayer by giving him the kind of peace which allowed him to write, "I have learned the secret of being content in any and every situation, whether well fed or hungry, whether living in plenty or in want" (Philippians 4:12).

He cares for you.

It's a beautiful promise that reminds you of God's intimate concern whether you're ill for weeks, disabled for months, or struggling within your marriage for years.

Grab hold of that truth and hang on. No matter what.

EXPECTATIONS

I'd just finished reading a riveting little book on prayer and couldn't wait to tell my husband about it.

As Ken helped me to bed that evening, I began excitedly to recount the new concepts and ideas that had throbbed in my thoughts all day long.

Naturally, I expected him to be as excited as I was.

He wasn't.

I'm not saying he yawned or nodded off as words of wisdom poured from my mouth. But then again, he wasn't sitting wide-eyed and awe-struck on the edge of the bed, either. He was . . . polite. Interested . . . but casual.

Well, that did it! I clammed up and had nothing more to say for the next hour. Finally, he noticed my cold shoulder and asked what the matter was. After a bit of coaxing I let it all spill out in tears.

That really got to him!

"Oh, Ken, you just don't understand," I told him. "I was so hoping you'd feel about these things—this book—like I do. I was so hoping you'd be as excited as I was."

I have to admit that Ken was kind and understanding—a little frustrated with me, but interested in talking it all out.

We both decided I had a problem with expectations. For that matter, so does he on occasion. Especially when I don't come unglued over how many fish he's snagged on his fishing trips. But he said something during that conversation that's really stuck with me.

"Joni, if I met all of your expectations, you wouldn't need God."

There's a lot of truth in that, isn't there? If our spouses were all we expected them to be, we wouldn't feel much inclination to depend on the Lord.

The Bible talks about expectations in Micah 7:

Put no confidence in a friend. Even with her who lies

in your embrace. . . . But as for me, I watch in hope for
the Lord (vv. 5, 7).

Elsewhere God's Word talks about not putting our trust in horses
or chariots or princes. It's so easy to do that, to let expectations
build.

But God doesn't want us to substitute anything or anybody
for Him. Not pastors or teachers, boyfriends or girlfriends, or
even husbands or wives.

So if your expectations have been crushed recently, and
you're disappointed, fearful that this person just isn't all you had
hoped he or she would be, maybe it's just God's way of reminding you to put your confidence in the Holy One.

He is able to meet your expectations. And unlike your
husband, wife, or close friends . . . He's perfect.

What Are the "All Things"?

And we know that in all things God works for the good of those who love him . . . (Romans 8:28).

You've seen it stitched in needlepoint on living room walls and over fireplaces. You've seen it inscribed on little magnets on refrigerator doors. It shows up now and then on key rings—and I've even noticed it hand-embroidered on a Teddy bear. You've probably memorized it in a couple of different translations.

Could it be we take Romans 8:28 for granted because it's so familiar?

I happened to be looking at the verse the other day when a question I'd never considered popped into my mind. I found myself wondering, *What did the apostle Paul have in mind when he wrote ALL things work together for good? What did he mean by ALL? What things could he have been thinking about?*

As I read on from Romans 8:28, I came across some surprising answers to those queries. Toward the end of the chapter, Paul seems to define what kind of "things" he is talking about.

The list isn't very pretty. It's not the kind of stuff you'd cross-stitch for your wall or embroider on a Teddy bear's tummy.

He starts with the word "trouble," and moves on from there to "hardship." After these, he pencils in "persecution," "famine," "nakedness," "danger," and "the sword."

Quite a list. And *these* are the things he believed God fit together for good in his life! He endured, confident that no amount of trouble or hardship could separate him from the love of God.

Somehow I can't picture Paul looking at the words of Romans 8:28 with a "ho-hum-I've-heard-it-all-before" attitude. I can't conceive of him becoming casual or nonchalant about such a wonderful truth. I get the distinct impression that items like nakedness, danger, and the sword kept him on his toes, kept him close to God.

What are the "all things" in your life today? What list could you come up with? No, "famine" might not lead your list. I'm guessing that "nakedness" or "the sword" might not crop up, either. It might not even include persecution. But you still have a list—and one as heartfelt to you as Paul's was to him.

Can you thank God for working all the circumstances and events of your life together for good?

Can you grasp the fact that today's list of troubles can never separate you from the love of God? Nor tomorrow's or tomorrow's or tomorrow's?

Don't let Romans 8:28 become like an old, worn pair of slippers. Don't shuffle through life with it. Don't let the truth of God's sovereign dealings in the lives of His children become some detached, abstract fact of life. Every time you encounter a new setback, struggle, or obstacle in your life, Romans 8:28 can bloom with new meaning.

It's as new as tomorrow's sunrise, and as fresh as your next hardship.

SUFFERING

*When God's Gifts
Come Wrapped in Pain*

6

SUFFERING
When God's Gifts Come Wrapped in Pain

Smoothed and flattened, the wrinkled sheet of wide-lined tablet paper lay in the center of my empty desk.

A crayoned sun in the upper right corner beamed five thick rays onto the happy faces of dancing flowers. A white house with two large windows and red shutters sat squarely in the middle. In front of the house, sitting in a chair with large, spoked wheels, was a girl with blonde hair, two pink circles on her cheeks, and a wide smile with neatly-lined teeth.

I smiled. A portrait of me?

Big blockish letters scrawled with a red marker bore the following message:

DEAR JONI,

I LIKE MY CAT AND I LIKE SCHOOL. I LIKE RE-CESS. WHEN I GROW UP I WANT TO HAVE A WHEELCHAIR JUST LIKE YOURS.

LOVE,

SHANNON

My smile broke into laughter.

Shannon is a healthy, active little girl who plays hopscotch, four-square, and "Mother, May I." She may not realize it, but she has absolutely no use for a wheelchair.

Try telling that to Shannon! A wheelchair would top her birthday list, more coveted even than a purple bicycle with pink and white streamers on the handles. As far as she's concerned, a wheelchair means *adventure*. A joy ride. An initiation into a very special Club.

Shannon hasn't a clue about the price one actually pays to join such a club. The pain. The paralysis. The disappointment. The heartache and hurdles. She discounts all that. She disregards the dark side, considering it not worth even knowing. All she desires is the chance to identify with me, to be like me, to know me. If that means having a wheelchair, then great—she'll take it!

It takes a child like Shannon to illuminate the meaning behind Paul's words to the Philippians:

> I consider everything a loss compared to the surpass-ing greatness of knowing Christ Jesus my Lord, for whose sake I have lost all things . . . I want to know Christ and the power of his resurrection and the fel-lowship of sharing in his sufferings, becoming like him in his death . . . (3:8, 10).

There's no better way to identify with Jesus—to be like Him and to know Him—than to gain initiation into the fellowship of His sufferings. Or as Shannon might say, "the Club."

Suffering has a way of taking life out of the abstract, out of the theoretical, making it painfully concrete. Lofty sermons from eloquent Bible teachers don't bring release to people locked in suffering. Ph.D. programs in ivy-walled seminaries don't deliver hope and comfort to those in deep pain.

When we suffer, we realize we are not handling theological ideas, we are rather being handled by a Person—the warm and intimate Person of the Lord Jesus. At other times, when life is rosier, we may slide by with knowing *about* Him, with imitating Him and quoting Him and speaking of Him. But only in the fellowship of suffering will we *know* Jesus. We identify with Him at the point of His deepest humiliation. The cross, symbol of His greatest suffering, becomes our personal touch-point with the Lord of the universe.

No one's asking you to beg membership in the Club as my little friend Shannon might. But there is something about her wonderful, wild abandon, her childlike trust, that must endear her to the Lord. All I ask is that you approach these next pages with a confident and hopeful smile . . . the smile of God's own dear child.

You don't have to choose suffering. You don't have to choose pain and humiliation. All you need do is choose God's will, as Jesus did on His cross. When you do, you'll be initiated into the Club—the fellowship of His suffering.

Membership has its privileges. Just ask Shannon.

Suffering: Friend or Foe?

Fire is a capricious friend. One moment it can be the best companion imaginable. An instant later it can turn on you with a vengeance.

I think back to a camping trip with my husband a couple of summers ago. I had looked forward to spending a cold evening huddled alongside a warm fire in the high Sierras. That's why I didn't mind when Ken left me by the firepit one night to fill his canteen at the creek.

It was such a pleasant night. The sky was huge and the stars seemed to hang so low. A slight breeze wafted the scent of pine right into our camp and the fire cracked and popped with amiable conversation. I sat mesmerized in front of the orange-red coals, feeling the heat on my cheeks, breathing in an aroma of burning oak.

The fire was my friend in the middle of a cold, dark forest.

Suddenly a wind came up and the whole picture changed. The flames vaulted higher and a choking cloud of smoke enveloped me. Unable to wheel myself away from the fire—or even cry out—I could only sit there, sputtering and coughing. Terrified, I watched the growing flames begin to lick around my feet. For a few awful seconds, I was afraid I would be seriously burned. There was nothing I could do about it.

At that moment, Ken returned, dropped his canteen and ran to push my wheelchair out of the path of smoke and fire.

I gained a new respect for our campfire that night. I learned how quickly a cozy mountain blaze can turn from friend to foe.

Fire. It's another one of those things with great potential for good—but also for bad. A campfire can barbecue tasty hamburgers one moment only to break its boundaries and attack a forest the next.

So it is with suffering. With profound potential for good, it can also be a destroyer. Suffering can pull families together, uniting them through hardship, or it can rip them apart in selfishness and bitterness. Suffering can file all the rough edges off your character, or it can further harden you.

146

It all depends. On us. On how we respond. By what we choose to do in the middle of our suffering. Do we use it—or let it use us? Do we go to God—or try to battle it out on our own?

Don't be surprised at the painful trial you are suffering as though something strange was happening to you. Remember the words of James: "Blessed is the man who perseveres under trial, because when he has stood the test, he will receive the crown of life that God has promised to those who love him" (James 1:12).

Suffering, which looks and feels like such a determined enemy, can be a valuable ally.

Only you can decide which it will be.

FINGERPRINTS

I had to be fingerprinted last month by an FBI agent.

No, I hadn't done anything wrong. I was being finger-printed because the president of the United States nominated me to serve on the National Council on Disability. What an honor! But after the nomination the FBI had to do a routine—and exhaustive—investigation on me. That meant fingerprints.

The polite G-man had problems with me. Yes, I cooperated to the best of my ability, but have you ever tried fingerprinting a lady who hasn't used her fingers in twenty years? Silly question. Obviously not. And I didn't think it would be any big deal. But that poor agent had one big headache trying to get prints off the pads of my fingers.

Finally, after four or five tries, he looked at me, shook his head and said, "Lady, I'm sorry, but you just don't have any tread on these fingers of yours."

I didn't know what he was talking about until he turned my hand so I could get a good, close look at my own fingers. He was right. I'd never taken the time to examine them before, but the pads of my fingers were super smooth with hardly any ridges at all.

I figured he had run into this sort of thing before, but he said, "No." The only folks without prints would be people who never used their hands. The agent went on to explain that ridges on fingers deepen with use. The hands of bricklayers, carpenters, typists, and homemakers who do a lot of dishes always have good prints. (I imagine diligent safecrackers would, too!)

Funny. I would have thought just the opposite. It seemed to me that hard work would wear off good fingerprints. But not so. Hard work enhances them.

I think it's the same for people who pour themselves out in service to the Lord. We tend to think Christians who charge full speed ahead, who give themselves in tireless service, will wear themselves thin. *They'll burn out*, we tell ourselves. *They'll dry up. They'll give themselves to the point of having nothing to give.*

I don't think so. Hard work—when done by the power and grace of God—enhances life. Our lives are built up in Christ as we serve Him, not worn down as we might think. Does a fruit tree injure itself by bearing bountiful fruit? Do we question the health of a vine loaded with grapes?

Look at the apostle Paul. He says in 2 Timothy 4 that he was being poured out like a drink offering. He had fought the good fight, he had finished the race.

But being used up like that didn't deplete him. Paul was not worn out. His spirit was as strong and great in the Lord Jesus as ever. He was never more complete. Life was never as full. And nobody had any trouble tracing his life, identifying his walk with the Lord.

So don't be afraid to give of yourself. If you're tempted to be a shrinking violet in Christ's kingdom, then you will surely shrivel, leaving no prints, no evidence, no means of identifying Jesus to others. No one will be able to trace your walk or follow your steps.

So get in there today and leave fingerprints—good, easy-to-identify fingerprints for God—on everything you do.

If you're ever on trial for being a follower of the Lord Jesus, make sure the prosecution has lots of evidence.

GOD'S DETAILED ARTWORK

One of the reasons I so love my artwork is that often God uses it to surprise me with some flash of insight, some fresh way of looking at His Word.

That happened to me recently when I was working on a rendering of the face of the virgin Mary for a Christmas design. She had to look like a young Jewish peasant, but I wanted to depict her in such a way that her royalty and nobility would shine right out of her face.

I gathered all kinds of photos of young Jewish women. I pored over fashion magazines to scrutinize cheekbones. I experimented with cool and hot and warm pinks. I even did a study of eyebrows. Then came revision after revision, erasure after erasure, test after test. I put Mary's face through everything, trying to attain the perfect, the ideal, the best rendering for the final painting.

Now, it's easy to set aside sketches I care little about or ideas that don't really excite me. I can even endure a slight mistake or two. But when I get truly excited about a piece, believe me, it gets bruised and battered with erasures and revisions. I push that rendering until it's just what I envision.

I'm convinced God deals with us in the same way.

For us to ask God to leave us alone or stop refining us, is to ask Him to love us less, not more.

Many of us think God "unloving" when He puts us through the test, pulling and pushing us, changing us into that complete idea of who He wants us to be. Could it be we're only considering a single dimension of His love—say, kindness, or gentleness—blowing it up as if it were the whole thing?

God's love is wider and deeper than that. It embraces constructive criticism, admonishment, correction, and spurring a person to do his or her best. If by love we mean keeping another from suffering or discomfort, then we say that God is not always loving. Neither is a doctor who sticks a needle into the bottom of a crying infant.

We *are* the objects of God's profound love and attention. Don't ask Him to stop perfecting and improving you. God has a final idea in mind and He's bringing you into completion— through revision after revision, erasure after erasure, sketch after sketch.

By doing that, He's not loving you less. Believe me, He's loving you more.

TEARS

Years ago when I was in the hospital, I noticed something very peculiar. Even though there was so much pain, so much disappointment in the lives of kids my age who were rehabilitating from accidents and injuries—even though you *knew* they were hurting—no one cried.

Sometimes I would lie awake in the middle of the night in my hospital room. I was so near tears, but I fought them back. For one thing, there was no one around to blow my nose and wipe my eyes. But I was also afraid. Afraid I would wake up my roommates and they would hear me. Maybe, just maybe, they would make fun of me the next day at physical therapy. So I kept my tears to myself.

That reminds me of something Chuck Colson once told me. "Men and women in prison don't cry," he said. "It's a sign of weakness, and weakness can be dangerous in prison."

Thankfully, things changed once I got out of that hospital and got my act together with the Lord. Getting closer to Jesus taught me weakness was something to *boast* in, something to delight in. Even the apostle Paul, who told us he gloried in his weakness, wrote to the Corinthian church with "much anguish of heart and many tears."

Then I learned about David—a real man's man, a warrior, and a king. He cried, too. The pages of the psalms are salted with this man's tears. In Hebrews I read of Jesus offering prayers and petitions "with loud cries and tears."

Big, burly Peter demonstrated that tears are only natural when one feels remorse or regret, like the time he heard the rooster crow the second time, recognized his sin, and wept bitterly.

Learning about these people in Scripture gave me the courage and confidence to cry! No longer were tears an embarrassment, a mark of weakness or shame.

What do your tears mean to you? The Bible tells us that "those who sow in tears will reap with songs of joy" (Psalm 126:5). God gives you a reason to hope, even though you find it tough to hold back the tears. Weeping won't last forever. But out of your tears of grief, love, or repentance, God brings a peace that *does* last forever.

Revelation 7:17 puts it this way: "For the Lamb at the center of the throne will be their shepherd; he will lead them to springs of living water. And God will wipe away every tear from their eyes."

It's ironic. In heaven, where I will be able once again to wipe my own tears, I won't have to.

BEAUTY OUT OF ASHES

The opening words of Isaiah 61 promise that God will bring beauty into broken lives. He will give beauty in exchange for ashes.

God will do this, the prophet tells us, that these very people might be called trees of righteousness, "a planting of the LORD" for His glory.

Those are comforting words for those pressed with limitations, those who know a daily struggle with profound personal obstacles. I know people like this. Broken men and women who have been given beauty for ashes; radiant believers who heighten God's reputation in a cynical world.

At a recent concert I watched members of a deaf choir stand up front to "sign" as the worship choir sang. The faces of those who were signing the words beamed with joy. You could tell they really *believed* the words to those hymns, even though they couldn't hear the sounds or the phrasing or the music.

I tried to be cool and not cry. But I just couldn't stop the flow of tears. I was deeply moved.

Sometime later I felt the same surge of emotion when I listened to the testimony of a man named David Ring. David is severely disabled with cerebral palsy and you have to listen intently to catch what he's saying. But in a thick, guttural voice, he spoke of the priority of giving thanks. His thoughts were threaded with Scripture, saturated with peace and joy.

Once again, my tears fell freely. Nor did I feel foolish or ashamed for crying.

Later on, however, I asked myself why I'd been so moved. I genuinely examined my motive. Was it pity? Was I simply feeling sorry for those people because of their disabilities?

No, I don't think so. I think I was responding to Isaiah's theme . . . it was the beauty. It was the lovely character, a right response, a solid witness, all born out of brokenness. Out of what could have been bitter ashes, God gave these people something more. They had become the planting of the Lord "for His splendor."

So the next time you find yourself deeply moved by the joyful perseverance of a Christian with a disability, thank the Lord for the grace that brings beauty out of ashes.

It's a tree of His planting, and the praise belongs to Him.

BEHIND THE QUICK SKETCH

My art instructor, an excellent craftsman, told me a compelling story about the benefits of diligent work.

Many years ago there was a famous Japanese artist named Hokusai, whose paintings were coveted by royalty. One day a nobleman requested a special painting of his prized bird. He left the bird with Hokusai, and the artist told the nobleman to return in a week.

The master missed his beautiful bird, and was anxious to return at the end of the week not only to secure his favorite pet, but his painting as well. When the nobleman arrived, however, the artist humbly requested a two-week postponement.

The two-week delay stretched into two months—and then six.

A year later, the nobleman stormed into Hokusai's studio. He refused to wait any longer and demanded both his bird and his painting. Hokusai, in the Japanese way, bowed to the nobleman, turned to his workshop table, and picked up a brush and a large sheet of rice paper. Within moments he had effortlessly painted an exact likeness of the lovely bird.

The bird's owner was stunned by the painting.

And then he was angry. "Why did you keep me waiting for a year if you could have done the painting in such a short time?"

"You don't understand," Hokusai replied. Then he escorted the nobleman into a room where the walls were covered with paintings of the same bird. None of them, however, matched the grace and the beauty of the final rendering. Yet, out of such hard work and painstaking effort came the mastery of Hokusai's art.

My art instructor's point was clear. Nothing of real worth or lasting value comes easy.

That's certainly true with my painting. As a Christian, I feel compelled to produce quality, the best I can do "as unto Him." To others it may appear that I sit in front of an easel and with a bit of quick inspiration render an effortless drawing. Let me tell you, behind what looks like spontaneous creativity and raw talent are hours of research, experiments, sketches, and color tests.

This must also be true of the canvas of our lives. Behind every attractive Christian life are things like discipline, prayer in the secret place, diligent study of God's Word, discreet acts of generosity, and obedience when nobody's looking.

We can't copy the world's slipshod way of looking at art—or life. If we want to have something of real worth and lasting value in our character, it won't come easy.

It never does.

CONTRASTS

An artist paints so that people might *see*.

You share beauty, elevate the imagination, inspire and challenge the senses—and seek to do it all without being blatant or obvious. The good artist will let the viewer discover truth for himself.

I think of a recent painting of a horse. As I painted, there were parts on that horse I thought especially attractive—parts I wanted the viewer to notice. Like that nice place where neck turns into chest. And those slender ankles. The tilt of the head was another point of interest.

As an artist I thought to myself, *How can I get the viewer to look at these places without being obvious?*

I noticed the horse's coat was a warm, golden color. What's the opposite color of gold? Violet, of course—a cool, dark contrast to the horse's coat.

That's what I'll do, I reasoned. *I'll lay this cool violet next to the special places on the horse. That will draw attention without being too conspicuous.*

As I worked on the horse's neck, I brushed a hint of violet alongside the gold. When placed alongside each other, these colors, subtle and mysterious, would attract your attention. Artistically, it was a successful attempt to have the viewer see what I wanted him to see.

God, too, is a Master Artist. And there are aspects of your life and character—good, quality things—He wants others to notice. So without using blatant tricks or obvious gimmicks, God brings the cool, dark contrast of suffering into your life. That contrast, laid up against the golden character of Christ within you, will draw attention . . . to Him.

Light against darkness. Beauty against affliction. Joy against sorrow. A sweet, patient spirit against pain and disappointment—major contrasts that have a way of attracting notice.

Your life begins to snap with interest. People notice you out of the corner of their eye—are drawn to you—without really understanding why.

They are, in fact, seeing what the Master Artist wants them to observe: Christ in you, highlighted against an opposing force of dark suffering.

You are the canvas on which He paints glorious truths, sharing beauty, and inspiring others.

So that people might see Him.

STIR THE FIRE

Could these words be yours?

Oh Lord, you deceived me . . . you overpowered me . . . I am ridiculed all day long; everyone mocks me . . . the word of the LORD has brought me insult and reproach all day long. But if I say, "I will not mention him or speak anymore in his name," his word is in my heart like a fire. . . .

That complaint was lifted right out of the Book of Jeremiah—from the lips of the prophet himself. Jeremiah was sick and tired of his "religious fanatic" label. He was fed up with the ridicule, rejection, and insults. The gossip was just too much for him.

Maybe you've said or thought something similar. Believe me, you're not the first to say to God, "Hey, I don't need this grief. I'm not going to bring up the Bible anymore. I'm not going to talk about God—and then maybe these people will lighten up!" Others have felt the sting and scorn to the point of saying, "I'm not even going to mention His name anymore."

I've felt that way. Shortly after the accident which paralyzed me, I took a stab at witnessing in the hospital. I talked about Christ with a couple of paraplegics who used to hang around the elevator in their wheelchairs at the end of my floor. They sat there, puffing cigarettes, disinterested, easily distracted. I tried telling them how God was helping me out of my own depression, but I could tell they were just tolerating me until I moved on. I could feel the resentment from those guys whenever I'd pass them by the elevator. I can remember thinking, *Fine. Telling people about God has only brought me more grief—as if I didn't have enough.*

I felt just like Jeremiah. Overpowered.

But there was something else about the prophet I identified with. After he had dumped his bucket on the Lord, crying out his hurt and resentment, he came back to a basic fact: "Lord, You know that even if I wanted to stop speaking Your Name I couldn't do it. Your Word is in my heart and it's burning like a fire."

I thank God He kept the fire burning in that prophet's heart. And in my heart, too.

Do you feel the fire—deep in your spirit? Even though the ridicule and gossip seem to throw a damper on it? Even though you feel shunned and rejected for talking about your Lord?

If you sense that burning, that nudging and urging to keep sharing God's Word, don't let it be quenched by your discouragement and fears. Stir the fire! Fan the flames! As Paul wrote to his friends, "Do not put out the Spirit's fire" (1 Thessalonians 5:19).

Even if those flames within you have dwindled to a single, lonely coal—just a faint glimmer—you still have the makings of a fire.

Don't let anybody throw water on it!

When God Says, "Enough!"

If you've ever wrestled with suffering, you know how your sense of timing can become warped. Sometimes circumstances seem to slide from bad to worse, from pain to deeper pain, from anxiety to agony. You begin to wonder when and if it will ever end.

God's Word—whether in little pieces or big chunks—can bring welcome perspective into times like these.

First, it's good to know that one day the curtain *will* be closed on all suffering and pain. There will come a point in time when the Lord God will say, "Enough!" In the end, God will create new heavens and a new earth where there will be no more tears or mourning or pain. The earth as we know it will simply pass from existence and be replaced.

The last book of the Bible gives a glorious preview of God's ultimate triumph over sin—and its counterparts like suffering and sickness and sorrow. It's all going to happen when God deals the final death blow to the devil and his angels. And when they're done away with, we have the assurance that suffering will fade from memory like a bad dream.

But in the meantime, God is able to use our suffering to glorify Himself. It is not wasted!

The Book of Proverbs says, "The LORD works out everything for his own ends—even the wicked for a day of disaster" (16:4). That means He has a plan and purpose behind your pain. Even the evil over which you have no control—evil men or evil schemes or injustice or iniquity—works mysteriously together in a pattern for your good (Romans 8:28).

Right now, however, you may be wondering what to do with all that time on your hands. Days that seem like weeks and minutes that seem like hours (how well I know!).

I can only say once again that the time is coming when victory, equity, and release are assured. Time, which allows for the existence of sin and evil, poses no threat to God and His character. Nor does it threaten you as His child, because freedom and fulfillment wait just over the horizon.

That's hope! Hope pure and simple. Listen to the triumphant ring of it—like the voice of great bells on a clear morning!

Listen, I tell you a mystery: We will not all sleep, but we will all be changed—in a flash, in the twinkling of an eye, at the last trumpet. For the trumpet will sound, the dead will be raised imperishable, and we will be changed.

For the perishable must clothe itself with the imperishable, and the mortal with immortality. When the perishable has been clothed with the imperishable, and the mortal with immortality, then the saying that is written will come true: "Death has been swallowed up in victory."

"Where, O death, is your victory?
Where, O death, is your sting?"

The sting of death is sin, and the power of sin is the law. But thanks be to God! He gives us the victory through our Lord Jesus Christ.

Therefore, my dear brothers, stand firm. Let nothing move you. Always give yourselves fully to the work of the Lord, because you know that your labor in the Lord is not in vain (1 Corinthians 15:51-58).

MYSTERY

A God
Beyond Comprehension

MYSTERY
A God Beyond Comprehension

Ever since I took
plane geometry in high
school, I've been itching to
understand the fourth dimension. Sound weird? Well, I've got
this thing about solving mysteries.

You see, I can explain the first dimension—a point in space.
The second dimension? A point moving through space creates a
line. The third dimension? A line moving through space creates a
solid. But the fourth dimension? Well, that's the mystery. I know
it has something to do with Einstein and $E = mc^2$, but even that's
pushing the limits of my brain.

Once a math teacher friend explained it to me. And for a
brief, wonderful, illuminating second I almost understood the
fourth dimension. But as fleetingly as it came, the answer—

enticing and inviting—vanished. I was thrilled beyond belief, yet baffled more than ever.

That's about as close as I can come to explaining my love/hate relationship with mysteries. Whether it's a perplexing mystery novel or a perplexing math problem, mysteries entice me even while they frustrate me.

Take, for instance, those mysterious paradoxes of Scripture.

We have a free will, yet we're predestined.

We're positionally perfect, but experientially imperfect.

We work out our own salvation, yet it is God who works His will within us. We're free in Christ, yet slaves to Christ.

Goodness, even the life of Jesus was a paradox—100 percent God and 100 percent man!

Every time I hear a paradox (something that seems contradictory and yet is quite true), I hanker to get my hands on it and shake some sense into it. Something about a paradox is tantalizing, yet irritating; it's a truth standing on its head to get attention, and I feel I must grab it and turn it right side up.

Something in me *has* to make enigmas understandable . . . puzzles, comprehensible . . . riddles, solvable . . . mysteries, known. No words describe the aching I feel when I almost, but not quite, have the answer; when I'm close, but not really, to understanding it all. It's a feeling not unlike "tasting" the answer to a difficult math problem!

It's like this: I have an itching to understand Colossians 1:26, which says we have been given "the mystery that has been kept hidden for ages and generations, but is now disclosed to the saints." Now, that's an enigma begging to be understood. And who among us can say we fully grasp that mystery?

Then there's 1 Corinthians 4:1, which assures us that we have been "entrusted with the secret things of God." I don't know about you, but that verse seems like a puzzle asking to be solved. Sure, we've been entrusted with the secret things of God; but which one of us knows all those secrets?

Or how about Ephesians 1:9? That verse tells us God has "made known to us the mystery of his will according to his good pleasure, which he purposed in Christ." To me, that verse is a mind-boggler craving to be unraveled. Yes, God has made known to us the mystery of His will; but is there anyone who can honestly say they understand that mystery inside and out?

See what I mean?

If you identify with me, then we're partners in puzzle solving. You and I are like-minded, Sherlock Holmes types. We are kindred spirits in solving the riddle of the sphinx. We're the sort of folk who must nail down those brain teasers. The aching you and I feel as we strain to "see through a glass darkly" makes us yearn to know the mysteries of God's will all the more.

Still, grasping God's mysteries is not unlike what Southey observed: "It's a perfect nonplus and baffle to all human understanding." Whether we like it or not, some of God's mysteries will forever remain mysteries. Others He has fully revealed. But there are yet others—tantalizing, inviting, alluring—which, every once in awhile, arrive at our doorstep bearing God's own signature: "This, My child, is for you. Won't you join Me in a treasure hunt?"

The puzzle pieces are spread before you. The clues of the mystery have been dropped, like hints, here and there. And God, as I have often said, has placed within us that age-old yearning of the spirit, that incurable urge to solve secrets and to delve into mysteries.

I hope you'll think of these next pages as puzzle pieces in this marvelous mystery of being "entrusted with the secret things of God." It's my prayer that you'll be thrilled by more than a few brief, wonderful, illuminating moments as you see those puzzle pieces begin to fit together.

Who knows? Maybe you'll discover that searching for the mystery of His will is more enticing, more exciting, more inviting, than you ever imagined.

Out of the Shallows

There's a river that flows past our old farm back in Maryland. The Patapsco meanders past fields and woods, parallels a railroad track, and eventually empties into the Chesapeake Bay.

As a little girl, I used to relish lazy, hazy summer afternoons on the banks of the Patapsco. While my sisters swam, I would wade and splash in the shallows, the cuffs of my pants rolled up past my ankles.

Not once did I venture out into the deep, unknown parts of the river. After all, I was awfully little—and that river was very big.

Yet I envied my sisters who were big enough to dive into the deep parts—places where they could swim and not even touch bottom. To me, my sisters seemed incredibly privileged.

How about you? Are you the sort of person who plays it safe, content with just getting your ankles wet? Or are you the adventurous sort who prefers to get in over your head?

I like to think of this Christian journey of ours as a river. A river of life. As I see it, the shallow places are the common habitat for all believers—the kind of faith and joy and hope we all take part in.

But there is a deeper realm of conscious union with Christ which is far from commonplace.

All believers see Christ. But not all put their fingers into the prints of His nails.

Not all believers put their hand in His side.

Not everyone has the high privilege of John to lean upon Jesus . . . nor of Paul to be caught up into a third heaven.

It is rare to find believers who live so outrageously for Christ that they leave the shallow places behind and dive into the free-flowing current.

"Most Christians are only up to their ankles in the river of life," wrote Spurgeon. "But few find life a river to swim in, the bottom of which they cannot touch."

It's a risky, wonderful place to be—out in those dark, inscrutable regions where you can't touch bottom no matter how deep you seem to dive. God invites us away from the safety of the bank, away from the measured security of the wading pools where the Christian life is almost easy.

You and I may begin in the shallows. But if we take God at His invitation, we dive deeper. Where we stop, no one has yet discovered . . . for there in the awful and mysterious depths of God there is neither limit nor border nor end.

STRONG MEDICINE

Nothing's worse than taking bad tasting medicine when you already feel sick and awful.

There's that white, chalky, liquid gunk you have to gulp down for diarrhea, or that goopy, pink potion for stomach cramps. They're downright nauseating. I usually have to quickly swallow something else just to keep the concoctions down.

Yes, the doctors and nurses assure me it's the best thing I can do, and I believe them. But it doesn't make the stuff slide down any easier.

Swallowing some of the hard sayings of Jesus can be a lot like ingesting that stomach-turning medicine. You *know* a particular truth in His Book is the best thing for your spiritual health . . . but that doesn't make it any easier going down.

It may be His advice to wait in the middle of an anxious, nail-biting family situation.

It may be His admonition to forgive a backbiting enemy.

It may be His quiet urging to pray compassionately and specifically for an in-law you just can't stand.

It may be His persistent reminder that all things are working together for your good, even though your toddler has to undergo critical surgery.

Some of that is simply hard to swallow.

Some of the Lord's disciples had this problem as well. At one point Jesus had some rather strong words for His would-be followers.

> On hearing [these words], many of his disciples said, "This is a hard teaching. Who can accept it?"

> Aware that his disciples were grumbling about this, Jesus said to them, "Does this offend you? . . . The words I have spoken to you are spirit and they are life" (John 6:60-61, 63).

The Lord Jesus admits some may find His words offensive. Even bad tasting. Nevertheless, His words *are* spirit and life. His advice, His counsel, His admonishments are life-giving medicine.

Still, acknowledging that fact won't make life into a picnic in the park. The family problems may get worse, your enemy may go on the rampage, and your in-law may get under your skin worse than ever.

But medicine is medicine. And even the hard words of Christ contain life and strength. Swallowing isn't easy, but it's the best option there is.

Healing makes all of life taste better.

WHEN GOD CONCEALS

"It is the glory of God to conceal a matter"
(Proverbs 25:2).

Goes against the grain a little, doesn't it?

We don't want matters concealed from us. Especially things that touch our lives. We want all the facts, the blueprint of God's design spread out on the table.

It is the glory of God to conceal a matter.

Consider the life of Amy Carmichael. She went to India in 1895, never realizing that country would become her home, the children of India her family. Nor did she know then that many beautiful, intelligent little girls in India were taken from their homes and trained to become temple women to satisfy the lusts of men in the worship of Hindu gods. She learned of this horrible custom when a seven-year-old who had escaped from a temple was brought to her house.

From that day on the Lord placed the desire in Amy Carmichael's heart to save these girls from moral ruin and train them to do the will of the heavenly Father.

Yet early on in her ministry, Miss Carmichael slipped into a pit, permanently crippling her leg. For the next *twenty years* she remained in bed, rarely leaving her room.

On the morning of the accident she had prayed, "Do anything, Lord, that will fit me to serve You better."

That accident was the answer. But in her confinement she went on to write thirteen books which have blessed generations of sufferers around the world.

It is the glory of God to conceal a matter.

"We speak of God's secret wisdom," Paul writes, "a wisdom that has been hidden and that God destined for our glory before time began" (1 Corinthians 2:7).

It is a glorious thing for a man or woman to be God-sufficient and not seek human explanations for His actions in his or her life. Even when those circumstances are totally mysterious.

As in the case of Amy Carmichael, the glory of the believer is absolute trust and confidence.

It is a glorious thing to know that your Father God makes no mistakes in directing or permitting that which crosses the path of your life.

It is the glory of God to conceal a matter.

It is *our* glory to trust Him, no matter what.

A FEW GOOD CLUES

Have you ever started reading a mystery novel only to quit in frustration less than halfway through?

Maybe there were too few clues—or the clues were absurd. The plot never thickened, the characters never developed. And the author seemed determined to leave the reader in the dark.

We give up on books like that because the mystery alone does not excite us. We can never get interested if we are left ignorant. To hold our attention, a good mystery novel must be sprinkled with facts, hints, information, clues.

God has mysteries, too. In Deuteronomy 29:29, Moses writes: "The secret things belong to the LORD our God, but the things revealed belong to us and to our children forever, that we may follow all the words of this law."

It's obvious God keeps many things secret. He conceals things so that He may be magnified through His people's trust in the midst of darkness and uncertainty.

Ah, but mystery alone could never excite our faith. No genuine spirit of trust in God could possibly spring out of ignorance. So, God does a marvelous thing in order that we might follow His words as expressed in Deuteronomy.

God alternates the hidden things with the revealed.

He keeps the mystery intact, but occasionally defines truth for us. He maintains secrets, but every once in a while, spells out some facts. It is that which excites our faith, stimulating us to trust Him all the more. He rouses and stirs our interest when He occasionally reveals reasons behind our disappointments or painful circumstances.

On the other hand, He tests and braces our faith when He chooses not to reveal the plot line. Truth, when veiled, calls out for a higher faith, a more childlike obedience than when the mystery is explained. When our trust in God stands the strain of great mysteries, He is glorified. So are we.

As for me, I'm happy the secret things belong to the Lord. I'm glad He doesn't explain everything. Otherwise, I wouldn't have the chance to simply trust Him. But I'm also pleased He chooses to reveal certain things. He gives clues. He gives facts. He hints of greater, even more marvelous things just over the horizon. And that stimulates more excitement to keep following Him.

I can't wait to see how it's all going to turn out.

IGNORING THE ODDS

You've had it happen to you. You're in a tough situation, you pray about it, and the Spirit of God answers—but *not* in the way you'd expect. You find the Lord Jesus asking you to handle your tough situation in a way you would have never expected!

Let's say it's a problem in the office. After much prayer, you sense the Spirit of God urging you to talk to your supervisor.

No way, Lord! you say to Him. *If I bring these things up before my boss, my job security goes down the drain!*

But despite your protests, the Spirit of Christ keeps prompting you to handle that tough situation *His* way—not in the manner you would normally choose.

Isn't that just like the Lord? *We* think God should have us manage a sticky job situation or domestic tangle one way (the "obvious" way, the "logical" way). After all, handling the matter with simple common sense improves your odds that everything will turn out right . . . right?

Wrong! God often calls us to ignore the odds, asking us to face our problems His way. And His way is sometimes most unorthodox.

Have you ever taken time to consider General Joshua's dilemma, described in Joshua 6? The Lord met with Joshua prior to the battle of Jericho, identifying Himself as "the commander of the army of the Lord."

What a relief, Joshua may have thought. *Now the Lord will lay out an infallible battle plan for attacking that powerful, walled city.*

Well, he got his battle plan, all right. But it certainly couldn't have been what he was expecting. Talk about an irrational, unorthodox way of handling a problem! Think about it. The Lord wanted Joshua and his army to march around Jericho for six days without saying a word. Then on the seventh day, they were to make the circuit seven times, listen for a trumpet blast, and then yell real loud!

Now I ask you, does that sound like common sense?

The book of Joshua, however, records that the Israelites followed God's instructions to a T. In spite of the risks, in the face of ridiculous odds, they simply did as the Lord had said. The result was one of the most dazzling victories in Israel's long history.

What is God asking you to do today that seems a little . . . unorthodox? Has the Commander of the Lord's army presented you with a highly unusual battle plan?

Ignore the odds and obey.

In the long run, you can't lose.

WHY BOTHER TO PRAY?

We delight in the knowledge that our God is sovereign, that He exercises control over the dates and details of our lives. But if things will be as they are going to be anyway, why bother to pray?

I used to worry and wonder over those questions when I was first injured, lying in the hospital. Christian friends assured me my injury was no accident, that it was part of His perfect plan.

That idea comforted me. But I remember lying awake long into the night thinking, *If God had all this in mind for me from the very beginning, what's the use of praying about my future? It's all in His hands anyway . . . what will be, will be.*

I was beginning to feel as though I had no part in God's will at all. He was in the driver's seat, I was simply along for the ride.

Somewhere along the line I finally summoned the courage to ask someone about prayer and God's sovereignty. Why should we expend the energy to pray?

I found there are several reasons—but the first is all we really need to know. *God has told us to pray.* It is a commandment, and if we love Him, we obey His commands.

But there is a second reason: *We pray because Jesus prayed.* Sometimes people will say the only reason for prayer is that *we* need to be changed. Yes, we do need change, but that's not the only reason to pray. Jesus didn't need to be changed or be made more holy. When He prayed He was communing with His Father. He thanked God. He praised Him. He asked for things. He requested power. He prayed on behalf of others. He asked that the devil be bridled. He asked His Father to prevent what was about to take place. He made clear His own will. He prayed as though His petitions had a definite effect on God's design.

In light of God's clear commands and our Lord's unmistakable example, it's obvious we believers "should always pray and never give up" (Luke 18:1). God does not want us to shrug our shoulders, shuffle our feet, and mutter "*Que sera, sera,* whatever will be, will be." On the contrary, Scripture makes it plain that we are *involved* with this life of ours—and the lives of others as well. Certain things simply will not happen . . . unless we pray.

How all of this fits into God's master plan and eternal design remains a mystery, but there is no mystery to the command. He says *pray continually* (1 Thessalonians 5:17).

That's reason enough.

ORDERING YOUR PRAYER

*Now, behold, I have ventured to speak to the Lord, although
I am but dust and ashes* (Genesis 18:27, NASB).

Dust and ashes.

I'm struck with Abraham's attitude in prayer—the attitude
that he had entered the treasure house of God and grasped
heaven in his arms. He knew that his prayer was a way of
embracing God. To think that he, Abraham, *had talked with God!* It
was almost as though he had mounted up with wings and entered the very dwelling place of his Lord. That thought itself was
enough to lay him low and cause him to say, "Lord, who am I?
I'm only a little pile of dust and ashes in Your presence."

It's been awhile since I've had that feeling in my prayer
times. Feeling like falling face-down before God because I've
glimpsed heaven. My prayers are more of a neat and orderly
arrangement—Adoration, Confession, Thanksgiving, and Sup-
plication all in a tidy row. I'm careful to follow a proper progres-
sion of praise and petition, almost as though I were moving
through an outline.

But when I look at Abraham's cry to God . . . a cry that had
nothing to do with a mere arrangement of suitable words . . .
when I consider his heart, his attitude, it's clear to me that
spiritually-ordered prayers consist of something far more than
clustering requests in a prim, prescribed fashion.

Spiritual prayers have to do with praying to Someone who
is real, with addressing ourselves to a God whom we cannot see
but who is, in fact, present with us. Spiritual prayers have to do
with conversing with the unseen Creator of the universe as
though He were standing visibly and terribly in front of us.

When we sense the reality of God's presence in that way,
we will be deeply humbled. We will be led by the Spirit to say
with Abraham, "I have ventured to speak to God, although I am
but dust and ashes." Our prayers will be something more than a
mechanical arrangement of words.

How long has it been since you've felt the dust and ashes? If talking to God doesn't strike you as being one of the most profound and extraordinary privileges imaginable, then perhaps Genesis 18 would be a good place to refresh your prayer life.

Only when we feel the dust and ashes can we enter the treasure house of God and embrace heaven.

MY THOUGHTS, GOD'S THOUGHTS

Sometimes the thoughts that fill my head are anything but high and lofty.

Take last night for instance. After Bible study, a few of the girls hung around and started talking as we sipped coffee.

You'd think we would have discussed what we learned from the study, right? No. Instead we debated the pros and cons of laundry detergent sold in see-through plastic bottles so you can tell when it's near empty. Oh yes—and then we discussed how somebody ought to put a clear plastic strip on the sides of toothpaste pumps so you can tell when they're running low. Let's see . . . we discussed the sale at a local department store, and why it is they decaffeinate coffee the way they do. Then we talked about news reports of what the First Lady has been up to.

Little wonder God said to Isaiah, "For my thoughts are not your thoughts, neither are your ways my ways . . . As the heavens are higher than the earth, so are my ways higher than your ways and my thoughts than your thoughts" (55:8, 9).

Somehow, I don't think God stays up at night worrying about laundry detergent or toothpaste pumps.

But let's take a moment to let those verses from Isaiah sink in. God's thoughts are so much higher than ours we can't even begin to comprehend the gap that must be bridged. And it *does* need to be bridged. If we're to walk and talk and feel with our Father, it stands to reason we must begin to *think* as He thinks. "Do two walk together unless they have agreed to do so?" (Amos 3:3).

Somehow, my thoughts need to be conformed to God's—or else I cannot hope to know Him or become like Him as He desires. But what can I possibly do to rise to His level? To elevate my thinking? To think His thoughts?

I can think as much as I please, but my thoughts—limited, finite, and so very human—still leave me on earth.

Ah, but all is not hopeless. Why? Because even though my thoughts cannot bear me up to the Almighty, *He* nevertheless is still thinking about me. The psalmist declares, "How precious to me are your thoughts, O God! How vast is the sum of them! Were I to count them, they would outnumber the grains of sand" (Psalm 139:17-18).

Do you get the picture? God thinks about us. *He* bridges the gap. He makes His thoughts available. He puts His thoughts into words we can understand, stooping to make Himself comprehensible. In fact, His thoughts are what the Bible is all about. They *are* within grasp. And when we lay hold of Him and His ideas, then and only then can we be drawn closer to Him.

Take some time for that today. Open your Bible to a passage such as one of those I've mentioned—Isaiah 55 or Psalm 139. You may be surprised at how heavenly-minded your thoughts really can be.

TRUTH: DISCOVERED OR REVEALED?

I well remember the drudgery of Algebra 1 back in junior high.

I've never been the mathematical, linear, or logical type. Always motivated to dig into music, art, history, and English, I've relished math like a trip to the dentist. Sure, I'd do my homework, study theory, listen in class, and try my hardest to understand what all my classmates apparently had little difficulty grasping. But somehow those funny little formulas never seemed to penetrate my gray matter.

But then came a day, a day still clear in my memory, when I discovered the truth of negative numbers. If you could have been sitting there in class with me, I just know you would have seen that big proverbial light bulb flash on over my head.

Ah-hah! Eureka! I was thrilled to finally be able to grasp all those equations and proofs.

Discovering truth after a long mental wrestling match is an exhilarating experience. But we shouldn't make the mistake of equating that sort of intellectual discovery with the experience of grasping the truth of God's Word.

We can participate in Bible studies, do our homework, grapple with all those doctrines, and try really hard to make sense of Scripture.

But if any light bulbs flick on in our thinking, it's probably not because we've "discovered" truth. More likely it has been *revealed* to us. By God.

Peter thought he made a great discovery when he answered Jesus' question with the words, "You are the Christ, the Son of the living God" (Matthew 16:16).

In the next verse, however, Jesus is quick to declare it was no artful detective work on Peter's part that brought him to that all-important truth. Peter did not discover who Jesus was. Christ said, "Blessed are you, Simon son of Jonah, for this was not revealed to you by man [that is, by human logic and surmising], but by my Father in heaven."

You can't unearth spiritual truth by the muscle of intellect or the brawn of our brains alone. God reveals these things to us. In fact, God goes so far as to say He hides these things from the wise and intelligent, revealing them instead to the childlike.

Perhaps our prayers today ought to be seasoned with the kinds of petitions that simply say, "God, reveal Yourself to me. Reveal Your truth in Your Word."

We may be surprised to find that all of our homework, study, listening, and trying will be effective. Not because we've put so much energy into it, but because our Father in heaven has chosen to pull back the curtain.

SIGNIFICANCE

*Believing God
Will Use Me*

SIGNIFICANCE
Believing God Will Use Me

Every morning Connie opens Diane's bedroom door to begin the long routine of exercising and bathing her severely paralyzed friend.

The sun's rays slant through the blinds, washing the room in a soft, golden glow. The folds of the covers haven't moved since Connie pulled them up around Diane the night before. Yet she can tell her friend has been awake for awhile.

"Are you ready to get up yet?"

"No . . . not yet," comes the weak reply from under the covers.

Connie sighs, smiles, and clicks shut the door.

The story is the same each dawn of every new day at Connie and Diane's apartment. The routine rarely changes. Sunrise stretches into mid-morning by the time Diane is ready to sit up in her wheelchair. But those long hours in bed are significant.

In her quiet sanctuary, Diane turns her head slightly on the pillow toward the corkboard on the wall. Her eyes scan each thumbtacked card and list. Each photo. Every torn piece of paper carefully pinned in a row. The stillness is broken as Diane begins to murmur.

She is praying.

Some would look at Diane—stiff and motionless—and shake their heads. She has to be fed everything, pushed everywhere. The creeping limitations of multiple sclerosis encroach further each year. Her fingers are curled and rigid. Her voice is barely a whisper. People might look at her and say, "What a shame. Her life has no meaning. She can't really do anything."

But Diane is confident, convinced her life is significant. Her labor of prayer counts.

She moves mountains that block the paths of missionaries.

She helps open the eyes of the spiritually blind in southeast Asia.

She pushes back the kingdom of darkness that blackens the alleys and streets of the gangs in east L.A.

She aids homeless mothers . . . single parents . . . abused children . . . despondent teenagers . . . handicapped boys . . . and dying and forgotten old people in the nursing home down the street where she lives.

Diane is on the front lines, advancing the gospel of Christ, holding up weak saints, inspiring doubting believers, energizing other prayer warriors, and delighting her Lord and Savior.

This meek and quiet woman sees her place in the world; it doesn't matter that others may not recognize her significance in the grand scheme of things. In fact, she's not unlike Emily in _Our Town_ who signs her address as:

Grovers Corners
New Hampshire
United States of America
Western Hemisphere
Planet Earth
Solar System
The Universe
Mind of God

In the mind of God . . . that's about as significant as you can get, whether you sit at a typewriter, behind the wheel of a bus, at the desk in a classroom, in a chair by your kitchen table . . . or lay in bed and pray. Your life is hidden with Christ. You enrich His inheritance. You are His ambassador. In Him your life has depth and meaning and purpose, no matter what you do.

Someone has said, "The point of this life . . . is to become the person God can love perfectly, to satisfy His thirst to love. Being counts more than doing, the singer more than the song. We had better stop looking for escape hatches, for this is our hatchery."[8]

It's my prayer that in these chapters, you will discover the significance that has been yours all along as a child of the King. You may not be able to know the meaning of every event, but you can know that every event is meaningful.

And you are *significant*.

A Deliberate Handicap

You probably know at least a few disabled people.

But did you ever think of the Lord Jesus in that category?

No, He didn't have a physical disability, but He did handicap Himself when He came to earth. Webster defines *handicap* as "any difficulty which is imposed on a superior person so as to hamper or disadvantage him, making that person more equal with others."

If we use that definition, then Jesus *was* handicapped. Think of it. On one hand He possessed the fullness of Almighty God, yet on the other hand He made Himself nothing. He emptied Himself, taking the very nature of a servant.

Talk about handicaps! To be *God* on one hand . . . yet to make yourself nothing. What a severe limitation! You would think it must have hampered the Lord, put Him at a disadvantage.

Jesus, Master Architect of the universe, designed planets and stars, galaxies and nebulae, pulsars and quasars. On earth He was a carpenter, limiting His design work to stools and tables.

Jesus, the eternal Word, spoke time and space into being. On earth He chose to speak to prostitutes, lepers, and sinners.

Jesus, the One who created the perfect bodies of Adam and Eve, despised pain and suffering as one of the awful results of the Fall. On earth, He endured backaches, cramped muscles, pangs of hunger and thirst. He sweat real sweat and cried real tears and bled real blood.

When I think of all this, it strikes me that these limitations just didn't "happen" to Jesus in the same way circumstances "happen" to you and me. The amazing thing is that Christ *chose* to be handicapped. I can't think of too many people who would make such a choice. I know I wouldn't.

But "since the children have flesh and blood, he too shared in their humanity so that by his death he might destroy him who holds the power of death" (Hebrews 2:14).

If you have a physical handicap, or maybe even an emotional or mental one, then you're not in bad company. If anything, you're in an elite fellowship with Christ Himself.

We had no choice over our handicap.

He did, and chose to be limited . . . so that He might set us free.

THE HIGH CALLING

Feel tucked away from what's happening at church these days?

Feel hidden, out of sight from all the goings on?

Maybe you even feel like you have some good talents and gifts . . . yet nobody seems to know about them but you.

Why is it that God doesn't put *you* on the front row once in a while? Why doesn't He give *you* a chance to display what you could really do for Him?

If I'm talking to you, let me paraphrase this advice from an anonymous writer:

> If God has called you to really be like Jesus in all your spirit, He will draw you into a life of crucifixion and humility . . . and put such demands of obedience, that He will not allow you to follow other Christians, and in many ways He will seem to let other good people do things which He will not let you do.
>
> Other Christians may push themselves, pull wires, and work schemes to carry out their plans, but you cannot do it; and if you attempt it, you will meet with such failure from the Lord as to make you sorely penitent.
>
> Others will be allowed to succeed, or having a legacy left to them or in having luxuries, but God will choose to supply you daily because He wants you to have something far better than gold . . . and that is a helpless dependence on Him.
>
> The Lord may let others be honored and yet keep you hid away in obscurity . . . because He wants to produce some choice, fragrant fruit which can only be produced in the shade.
>
> God will let others be great but keep you small. He will let others get the credit for the work you have done, and this will make your reward ten times

greater when Jesus comes. The Holy Spirit will put a strict watch on you and rebuke you for little words and feelings which other Christians never seem distressed over.

So make up your mind that God is infinitely sovereign and has the right to do as He pleases with His own. And He will not explain to you a thousand things which may puzzle you. God will take you at your word, and if you absolutely sell yourself to be His slave, He will wrap you up in a jealous love.

Settle it forever, that you are to deal directly with the Holy Spirit. Now when you are so possessed with the living God that you are, in your secret heart, pleased and delighted over this peculiar, personal, private jealous guardianship and management of the Holy Spirit over your life, you will have found the vestibule of heaven.

"NAMELESS" PEOPLE

Has anybody referred to you as "Mr. So-and-So"? As if he or she either couldn't quite remember your name—and didn't much care?

Most of us have had that dubious distinction somewhere along the line, labeled "Miss What's-her-name" or "old What's-his-face." Frankly, it hurts to think that someone can't or won't extend the simple courtesy of remembering your name.

But take heart, all of you "so-and-so's" and "such-and-suches." You are remembered! And you're in fine company. Consider all those good, nameless people in the Bible.

In Hebrews 11, after the writer pinpoints sixteen well-known saints, he adds that he hardly has time to tell about Gideon and Samson and Samuel and David and the rest of the prophets.

Then he goes on to talk about "the others." Unnamed folks who had just as much faith as those biblical celebrities in the chapter. In fact, the writer claims that the world wasn't even worthy of this group of "what's-their-names." He closes out the chapter by saying that all of these "what's-their-faces" were commended for their faith. Then, after penning this marvelous book of Hebrews, the writer neglects to sign his own name!

There are other anonymous players. In Matthew 26 Jesus directs His disciples to make preparations for the Passover. He says, "Go into the city to a certain man and tell him, 'The teacher says . . . I am going to celebrate the Passover with my disciples at your house'" (v. 18).

Beg pardon, Lord? We didn't catch the name. Who in the world is this "certain man"? History will never know. In fact, so nameless was he that the Greek reads: "Go into the city and tell Mr. So-and-So . . ."

Let's not forget the nameless people who provided the donkey for Jesus to ride in His triumphal entry into Jerusalem. And yes, the nameless person who provided solace and rest to the Master and His disciples by offering his garden . . . a quiet little spot called Gethsemane.

Perhaps you are tempted to feel like a "nobody" in the Kingdom of God. Your talents are few, you're still looking for your spiritual gift, people frequently mistake you for someone else, and you're half convinced you'll never make a name for yourself. Anywhere. Ever.

Ah, be encouraged, friend. Even though your name may not roll off the tip of many tongues, God truly remembers who you are. He not only knows your name (first, last, and middle), He knows the exact number of hairs that grace the top of your head. He knows your heart, your worries, your dreams, and your deepest longings. As the Lord told Israel, your name is inscribed on the palms of His hands.

Furthermore, there's no "what's-his-name" or "who's-a-which" written down in the Lamb's Book of Life. That's *your* name written there. A name well known in heaven. And well loved.

WHEN SKEPTICS THINK TWICE

Hemingway was a swashbuckling adventurer who played and worked with reckless abandon—writer, hunter, fisherman, and soldier of fortune. It was Hemingway who coined the phrase, "Courage is grace under pressure." The author probably arrived at that conclusion after observing someone suffering with resilience and dignity.

Such a person would have caused him to stop and think twice.

I remember a long-ago friendship with an atheist, a one-time philosophy professor at Georgetown University. It all began when I took issue with a statement he made: "God is D-O-G spelled backwards."

I wasn't about to let that one slip by, and so began an earnest and lively series of discussions. Finding so many things to disagree over where it concerned the God of the Bible, I was surprised that our times together continued. Our friendship would have ended sooner than it did, but one thing kept prolonging our conversations: My wheelchair and my response to it.

Once, while feeding me Chinese food with his chopsticks, he paused. "This," I recall him saying as he rubbed his chin and looked at my wheelchair, "I can't explain."

My response to my disability made him think twice about God.

Sometimes skeptics will look at a Christian who suffers with grace and dignity, and try to deny that God is the real source of that individual's inner peace.

To the nonbeliever, all this talk about heaven, God, and the joy of the Lord is escapism, a mental cop-out, a refusal to face reality. From time to time I've been accused of using faith in God as a psychological crutch.

When this happens, I merely point to the facts: It's hard enough for someone who's always been an indoor bookworm sort of person to adjust to life in a wheelchair. But most people—even those skeptics—agree that it's even harder for someone such as myself who's been very active. Believe me, when I was on my feet, I was always on the go, rushing ninety miles an hour from one event to the next. But now I operate on super slow speed because of my severe paralysis.

No mere set of do's and don't's, no speculative religious philosophy dreamed up in my head, no belief in a vague and mushy all-Supreme First Cause could sustain me in this wheelchair. Nor could any such psychological mishmash actually release me to *rejoice* in my condition. Either I must be insane, or there is a living God behind all of this—a Personal Deity who is much more than just a theological axiom.

He is alive, active, and demonstrates His presence in my life again and again . . . sometimes in spite of myself. And *this* has made people think twice about Him.

When Christians suffer with grace under pressure, people who observe even casually are forced to consider the fact of a God able to inspire such loyalty.

The way you and I handle our big and little trials makes the world pause in its frantic, headlong pursuits. Our godly response to those obstacles and perplexities in our lives literally kicks the psychological crutches right out from under the skeptic. The unbeliever can no longer refuse to face the reality of our faith.

So hang in there, Christian. Your joyful obedience is a phenomenon that simply can't be explained away.

For you, and a watching world, courage is spelled G-O-D.

IN THE CORNER OF A FIELD

He drew His followers apart from the frantic pace of ministry and led them to a quiet corner of a field. He stopped, perhaps
knelt, and touched a seemingly insignificant wildflower.

Observe how the lilies of the field grow . . . (Matthew
6:28, NASB).

I can imagine the disciples shooting glances at each other as
they got down on their knees with the Master among those tiny
flowers. *Now what?* Can't you see big, burly Peter dropping to his
knees, peering self-consciously at the fragile blossoms? Most of
those men had probably never given much thought to simple
field flowers. It had certainly never dawned on them to stop in
the middle of a hectic day to *observe* the frilly little things.

But the Lord knew what He was asking.

*Look at this, Peter. Come closer, Philip. Kneel down a minute,
Bartholomew. Over here, Matthew. Do you see this little lily? It's never
worked a day in its life. Doesn't know a thing about the morning
commute. But gentlemen . . . even Solomon in all his storied splendor
couldn't hold a candle to the glory of this tiny bloom. And if that's how
God dresses a humble flower in the corner of a field, don't you think
He'll meet your needs, too?*

Lilies—and the way they grow—can teach us something
about the way the Lord wants *us* to grow. You may be one of
those tucked away out of the sight of others, feeling like you're
stuck in some corner of a field. There you are, bobbing in the
wind . . . quiet, little insignificant you, unseen by most and
unappreciated by many.

But grow you do. Why? Because instead of all the "laboring
and spinning and toiling"—which, as Jesus pointed out, does not
help one grow in the least—you, like a flower in the field, simply
turn your face toward the Son.

It is His light which causes you to grow.

It is in Him, not in busy activities, that you find your
strength.

His grace and life are the source of your increase.

Have you considered the way a wildflower grows? Peering into its dainty face can remind you Who's really in control . . . the One who saw fit to place you in that quiet corner of your world.

The God who clothes the wildflowers and makes them grow is the Father who cares for every intimate detail of your life.

That's worth kneeling down to consider.

Our Bodies, Like Tents

When we went beach camping as kids, I thought living in a tent was the ultimate adventure.

Sand on the canvas floor? Who cares! Mosquitoes? Just get out the mosquito netting. Rain? Break out the tarps and pull down the canvas flaps. Dirt? Hey, a little dirt never hurt anybody.

Hey, living in a tent is *fun*.

Now, thirty some years later, it's a different story. Ken and I still enjoy camping, but I can only take it for so long. For some reason, tent camping seems to get a little more strenuous with each passing year. Sand, mosquitoes, dirt, rain? *You can have it* I say to myself after four or five days.

Maybe that's why the apostle Paul (himself a part-time tentmaker), likened living in these bodies of ours to living in a tent.

A tent is only temporary. We can only take it for so long. And with each passing year, we find living in these bodies of ours more strenuous than the year before.

Aren't you glad we won't always be "groaning and burdened" with these patchwork tents of ours, as Paul says in 2 Corinthians 5?

When I think along these lines, Steve Coyle's story comes to mind. Steve, who lived in Hawaii, went swimming for an hour each morning. One day a diving accident badly bruised his spinal column. He recovered from that mishap, but just three months later had another accident which left him a quadriplegic. Even so, Steve never complained about his disability. He always managed to work in some words of praise to the Lord in all his conversation.

I wish the story got better from there, but the truth is, Steve then developed cancer. He suffered greatly, and after losing over eighty pounds, went to be with the Lord. How he must have grown weary of his tent!

Shortly before he died, Steve wanted to record some of his thoughts in verse. He entrusted these lines to a nurse friend.

When I looked upon the days gone past,
I'd thought this tent was built to last.
For I'd stood it on some rocky ground
where stormy winds couldn't beat it down.

And with much pride and my own hand,
I put my tent on shifting sand
where pegs pulled loose and my tent did shake,
but I was young and I could take
the unstable world that I was in
I'd just up and move again.

So for many years I went this route,
shifting this old tent about.
Till one cold day when my mind grew clear,
this tent had an end and it might be near.
So with much fear (such a heavy load)
I looked for the One who made this abode.

Yes, the Tentmaker, He'd surely know
where one such rotting tent should go
to have this canvas revitalized,
to have these poles and pegs re-sized.

I went to Him on bended knees
begging Him, "Oh tentmaker please!
Restore this tent I thought would last,
this canvas house that went so fast."

He looked at me through loving eyes
and merely pointed to the skies.
"Please don't grieve over some old tent,
old canvas walls that have been spent.
For this mansion that's been built by Me
will last you for eternity."

With that assurance, Steve Coyle gladly broke camp and
moved on.

MORE WITH LESS

God has a way of accomplishing more with less.

For instance, even though I'm much more limited and restricted than in the days when I was on my feet, God is accomplishing much more through my life now than He did then.

I'm reminded of that fact every time I look at a certain painting of mine . . . my first painting of a horse.

When I was a teenager, horses preoccupied me. If I wasn't riding and exercising them I was brushing and feeding them. I spent so much time with horses in those days I'm surprised it took me so long to finally paint a picture of one of my favorite subjects. How long? *Sixteen years.*

To get started on that painting, I gathered and studied scores of horse photographs. As I made my initial sketches, I pieced together my own "original" horse from all those shots, taking bits of information from a multitude of sources. After coming up with a satisfactory composition, I mixed my colors. I wanted him to be a dapple gray with splashes of sunlight on his coat through the shade of trees.

As I began painting, I really tried to get into the movement and feel of the animal. I had to reach down within myself, my memories, and pull out everything I knew about horses in order to capture one on canvas.

Frankly, I was surprised to discover how much I remembered.

Though I haven't had feeling in my hands for years, the sensations came back to me . . . my hand smoothing down the shiny coat . . . the touch of my fingers braiding the mane . . . the soft, nuzzly feel of a horse's nose. All these perceptions were as clear in my mind as if I'd taken this imaginary gray of mine out for a ride yesterday.

The painting turned out fine. I felt I was able to create a special, very individual kind of horse in a lovely setting.

I haven't ridden a horse in many years. I'm rarely around a stable. It's been a long time since I've known the touch of a horse's coat. But I think I know far more about what makes up a horse now than I ever did when I was on my feet. I certainly know that I can paint one much better than I ever did in my past. With patience, contemplation, persistence, thought, imagination —and a heart that's learned quietness—I am able to do much more with far less.

I wonder if we honestly realize the rich resources which God provides when He takes away our health or certain coveted abilities.

We may think we could do far more with more.

But God knows He can do a great deal more in our lives with a good deal less.

"But What About HIM?"

As my bare feet positioned themselves on the edge of the raft one hot July afternoon in '67, it never occurred to me that the murky waters of the Chesapeake Bay into which I was about to plunge concealed a shallow bottom.

I should have known better. I should have checked the depth. But those innocent-looking waters lured me into a trap which broke my neck and cost me the use of my hands and legs for the rest of my life.

There is an innocent-looking trap awaiting each person who suffers. The trap isn't a body of water. It's an attitude. The temptation to compare yourself with others who seem to have it easier than you.

Take a few dives into this destructive frame of mind, and you're liable to end up paralyzed—by self-pity. Haunted by a bitter, restless spirit. Robbed of hope, contentment, and joy.

I'm not sure which was worse during the early years of my life in a wheelchair, the paralysis of my body or the paralyzing effects of my self-pity. I couldn't even visit a shopping mall because all I could do was compare myself with the young women walking by—their clothes hanging on them so nicely. Even watching my best friends model an outfit for me made my face flush with envy.

Back then, I never considered such self-pity to be the terrible offense to God that it actually is. In view of my circumstances, I figured God would "understand" a little self-indulgence.

That assumption changed when I encountered a story in John, chapter 21.

Jesus had just told Peter to expect a martyr's death years in the future. That was hard enough for the apostle to swallow, but what made it even harder was Jesus' silence about John. Even though John was standing there listening to it all, Jesus never spoke a word about the fate awaiting *him*. Peter sized up the situation and judged that John was getting the better deal.

Wait a minute, here! Peter probably thought. *Wasn't John the one who got to sit next to Jesus at the supper? Wasn't John the one who seemed especially buddy-buddy with the Master? And now is Christ really about to let John off with an easy out on some sunny Mediterranean isle?*

It was too much for Peter to keep inside. "What about *him*?" he blurted, pointing to John.

The Lord's answer must have shocked Peter. He might have been expecting some kind of reassurance. Something like, "Don't worry, Peter. I'll be with you through whatever. Everything's going to be all right."

Instead Jesus delivered a stern rebuke. He allowed no room for indulgence . . . no temporary luxury of a "poor me" attitude.

"Look," He said in essence, "if it's My will that John lives until I come again, what's that to you? What I have planned for John is none of your business."

Rather harsh words for Jesus to use with a man facing martyrdom, wouldn't you think? Was the Lord right in being so stern? Didn't Peter, arguing for "equal rights," have good reason to doubt the goodness of God's plan?

That passage taught me a lesson as I weighed its implications. Jesus will deal harshly with self-pity because He knows it only magnifies a man or woman's misery. Comparing my situation with others and demanding equal rights is no better than doubting the goodness of God's plan for me—and ultimately, the goodness of God Himself.

Are you paralyzed? Maybe not in body, but in attitude? You don't have to choose the murky, hazardous waters of self-pity. Let me post a sign that might save your life for His service: DANGER! DON'T DIVE HERE!

Nothing to Give?

When I was growing up on a farm in Maryland, Christmas began the day after Thanksgiving and ran nonstop through December 25. There were parties and plays, dances and dates, decorating, baking, and shopping.

Especially shopping.

My sister and I would traipse through stores by the hour searching for the perfect gift for everyone on our lists. One Christmas I looked for days before I found an Angora sweater for Jay—light peach, size 36, with embroidery at the neck. For Mother, the ideal gift may have been a special dress. For Dad, a horse bridle with silver trim. It was exhausting, but what fun to see their faces on Christmas Eve when we opened presents.

Then came the 1967 swimming accident that left me paralyzed. I spent Christmas that year in a Baltimore rehab center. What a contrast. There I was, a seventeen-year-old girl brimming with mental energy—longing to celebrate Christmas in the same frantic, event-filled way the Earecksons always celebrated. Yet I couldn't even move from my bed without help.

One of the things that depressed me most that year was my inability to go out and shop for my friends and family. I felt I had nothing to give as Christmas drew nearer.

I cried with an inner rage, blaming God for my predicament. But a friend who visited daily with me in the hospital read a familiar verse out of the Bible: *"For God so loved the world that He gave His only begotten Son . . ."*

Those words from John 3:16 hit me as never before.

God's best gift to humankind, the one that proved forever just how much He cared for each of us, was a gift of *Himself*. His only Son. Likewise, I realized that my best gift to Him and those I loved was . . . me.

The next day when it came time for occupational therapy—an experience I had previously dreaded—I asked a therapist to bring me one of the plaster candy dishes like some of the other patients had been decorating. Next, I asked for a paintbrush and some red and green paint.

Gripping the brush awkwardly in my teeth, I began to daub at the oakleaf-shaped dish. Few brushmarks landed where I aimed them. I slopped green where I really wanted red. But it was the best I could do.

When the dishes were finished and glazed, I had them wrapped and gave them as presents to my family and friends. They weren't store-bought gifts, or very pretty, but they were my best. Gifts of myself.

When life is reduced to its essence, those are the gifts that are treasured and remembered.

PERSEVERANCE

*God's Partnership
in Life's Marathon*

PERSEVERANCE
God's Partnership
in Life's Marathon

I've seen him in the hills above town, early in the morning, running in line with his high school teammates.

Most days after school Clay does volunteer work at our office, packing boxes and stuffing envelopes. But now that it's cross-country season, he's out on the roads and trails, pushing his body to its limits.

Keeping me updated, my young friend tells me his school has already won several meets this year. In one race, he placed tenth in a field of sixty-five harriers.

When I had the chance, I asked Clay a question that's been on my mind since he joined the team.

What's the most difficult part of a long-distance run?

I've heard some say it's that first mile or so. Your muscles feel tight and the long course seems to stretch out forever before you.

Others have told me it's that final stretch that's the killer. You're exhausted, your limbs feel like wood, and you're scarcely able to lift one blistered foot in front of the other.

But my young friend immediately had a different answer. The worst part of a cross-country run, he told me, is neither the beginning nor the end. It's the middle—the long and lonely tramp, those long minutes when you're out of range of those cheering voices at the start and finish lines. It's that long, gray, middle distance that saps your strength and your will.

My friend quoted a verse that helps him when he hits that mid-point in the race.

> Those who hope in the LORD will renew their strength . . . they will run and not grow weary, they will walk and not be faint (Isaiah 40:31).

Some say it's the mid-point blues that the prophet had in mind when he gave this prophecy to Israel. As Israel was released at last from the long captivity, God promised He would go with them on the long trek from Babylon to Jerusalem. And yes, He would be with them when they hit that desolate mid-point of the journey. When the way back was as far as the way forward. When the desert sun washed the landscape of color and the destination seemed a lost and distant thing . . . a mirage in the sand.

Have you been there?

Ever feel like you're in the middle of a long stretch of the same old routine? The beginning of the Christian life was exhilarating. Lots of smiles and handshakes and encouragement. Your emotions soared. And the end? Well, it's going to be wonderful meeting Jesus face-to-face.

But now . . . you're in the middle. There are miles behind you and miles to go. You don't hear any cheers or applause. That first shot of spiritual adrenaline wore off a long time ago. The days run together. So do the weeks. Your commitment to simply keep putting one tired foot in front of the other begins to flag and fade.

Ah, but the promise in Isaiah is just as true now as then. If we walk in the Spirit, our strength *will* be renewed. We will run and not be weary. Even in the long, gray, middle distance, we will walk and not be faint.

The writer of Hebrews also had some good words for fainting saints. In chapter 12 he wrote, ". . . Let us throw off everything that hinders and the sin that so easily entangles, and let us run with perseverance the race marked out for us. Let us fix our eyes on Jesus, the author and perfecter of our faith" (v. 1-2). A little later in the chapter he offered some encouragement for those with sore legs and feet—those who seemed on the verge of dropping out of the race.

> Therefore, strengthen your feeble arms and weak knees. Make level paths for your feet, so that the lame may not be disabled, but rather healed (v. 12-13).

It won't be long until the race is over. The tape is just ahead . . . around the bend, over the hill, and through some trees. Believers who have gone ahead crowd the grandstands, awaiting your triumphant finish.

Yes, the middle part of the race is difficult. Sometimes excruciating. But every step brings you closer to that finish line. Fix your eyes on the One who awaits you there. You're halfway home.

I pray that the thoughts in this chapter will help you keep on course.

KEEPING IN STEP

Since we live by the Spirit, let us keep in step with the Spirit (Galatians 5:25).

That's good advice for those of us who try to live too far ahead in the future.

We book our calendars through June before the first March daffodils poke through the frost. Our minds range far and wide over distant, misty horizons and our eyes strain to peer over hills and around corners. When obstacles loom in the path of our carefully plotted course we think of them as "barriers" to our goals and objectives.

In a society where we're pushed forward so quickly, we tend to forget it's the *moment* that counts.

That's why I love verses like Galatians 5:25. How in the world can we expect to live by the Spirit if we seek to move through life mile by mile rather than step by step? Our walk in the Spirit is to be just that . . . a walk, not a sprint.

When we get ahead of ourselves, we end up disregarding the present . . . the people around us right now . . . the opportunities immediately at hand.

When we get ahead of ourselves, we make the mistake of ignoring the specifics. Specifics like sin. And instant obedience. Preoccupied with future agendas, we don't have the energy to engage in that daily, moment-by-moment struggle with the sinful, selfish habits that dog our feet.

When we're keeping in step with the Spirit, He can pinpoint those areas in our lives that need change. But when we get ahead of Him, trying to take life in leaps rather than steps, we tend to gloss over the daily obstacles and challenges.

Our prayers become too general.

Our Bible reading becomes merely a 10K run that needs to get finished.

Our obedience centers around a lot of outward actions rather than a daily cleansing.

Jesus becomes a "goal" rather than a Person to whom we relate moment by moment.

Heaven gets placed on a shelf in the faraway future rather than on a meal table marked "today."

So what I say to you, I say to myself. *Slow down.* Take time to chew on a few meaty words from James the apostle . . . and Jesus the Lord:

> Now listen, you who say, "Today or tomorrow we will go to this or that city, spend a year there, carry on business and make money." Why, you do not even know what will happen tomorrow. What is your life? You are a mist that appears for a little while and then vanishes. Instead, you ought to say, "If it is the Lord's will, we will live and do this or that." As it is, you boast and brag. All such boasting is evil (James 4:13-16).

> Seek first his kingdom and his righteousness, and all these things will be given to you as well. Therefore do not worry about tomorrow, for tomorrow will worry about itself. Each day has enough trouble of its own (Matthew 6:33-34).

The Christian faith is meant to be lived moment by moment. It isn't some broad, general outline—it's a long walk with a real Person. Details count: passing thoughts, small sacrifices, a few encouraging words, little acts of kindness, brief victories over nagging sins.

If you're going to walk with Me, the Spirit seems to be saying, *pay attention to the present.*

If you keep running ahead, you may find yourself walking solo. And that's not only dangerous, it's lonely.

By Love Constrained

Not long ago I flew into Indiana for a speaking engagement at a church. One of the pastors met me at the airport, escorted me to a station wagon, and whisked me across the lush, summer countryside.

As we discussed his church, I often glanced out the window at the beautiful fields passing by. I commented on what a lovely area it was. Great farmland. Rich acres of all sorts of vegetables. The countryside seemed especially productive.

"Wasn't always like this," my driver replied with a smile. "At one time this whole area was marshland. One big swamp."

The pastor had my complete attention as he went on to describe how a nearby river would overflow its low banks every spring, rendering all of that prime land useless. To counter that annual dilemma, the state undertook a vast engineering project to build up the river banks throughout that vulnerable area. As a result, the waters of the river were controlled and channeled, freeing up rich acres of productive farmland.

He compared what happened there to the love of God in our lives. He mentioned Paul's words in 2 Corinthians 5:14, (KJV): "For the love of Christ constraineth us. . . ."

"I'm glad you brought that up," I told him, "because I've never really known what 'constraineth' actually means."

He laughed. "Well, Joni, as I understand it, constraining means to *press in* . . . in order to *push forward*. When that river was pressed in on each side by reinforced banks, the flow of water was constrained, or pushed forward, resulting in more productive farmland.

"It's the same with us," he went on. "Sometimes God in His love brings about circumstances which seem to press in on every side—walled situations or high hedges where we feel closed in. Yet God allows these crushing pressures to ultimately push us forward and make us more effective, more productive. Though we may not like it, the trials press us and push us in a better direction—a direction God wants us to head."

I've never forgotten that word picture from my Indiana friend. The Lord brings it back to my mind on those occasions when the walls of my world seem to be closing in on me.

Is it like that for you today? Do you feel barricaded and pushed upon from every side?

Could it be that God is beginning to press you in . . . for the purpose of compelling you forward? Could it be that those hardships you're experiencing are evidences of the constraining love of Christ?

It may be that your life hasn't been as fruitful or productive as you know it might have been. Wandering without direction, you sense wasted time, wasted energy. Instead of a rich field of grain, your life seems more like a stagnant swamp.

Thank God for His sovereign intrusion into your life! Thank Him that He loves you too much to let you wander, wasting your life and energies. Your circumstances—even the pushing, squeezing, distressing ones—are part of His plan. It's a plan to make your life more productive than you ever dreamed possible.

That's divine engineering at its best.

ALL LIFE IS SPIRITUAL

I'm not what you call "computer literate," but I can manage my way around documents, files, editing formats, and window directories. I love it! Working away on my little Macintosh, I get swept up in a passion to edit, cut, and paste *everything* into little files and compartments.

This piece of information goes here. That byte of data goes there. This goes on the hard disk. That goes on the back-up floppy.

Trouble is, it's sometimes difficult to turn off that computer mentality after I shut down my machine and head home. I find myself wanting to file, sort, and compartmentalize life in general.

Let's see . . . this goes in the "everyday" folder, that goes in the "spiritual" file . . . this is common stuff, this is sacred stuff. . . .

Do you ever get caught up in that kind of thinking? For instance, we sometimes mistakenly think that only gospel hymns—and not classical music pieces—are spiritual. Or we think that only *Pilgrim's Progress*—and not *Treasure Island*—is spiritual.

We get the idea that "full-time Christian service" applies to staff workers at Youth For Christ, but doesn't apply to the CPA who walks with Christ, works hard, and keeps a straight ledger.

Frankly, ALL of life for the Christian can be spiritual. We need to understand that *every* good gift—whether a beautiful piece of music, a time-honored piece of literature, or even an opportunity to be a witness in a so-called secular area of employment—comes from the hand of a gracious and giving God.

In Him we move and breathe and have our being. That means everything we do and say and touch can have spiritual significance. Eating roast turkey with homemade gravy—and fresh California asparagus—can be something which glorifies God if done with a grateful heart. Relaxing under the strains of Bach or Vivaldi can bring glory to God if we consider such pleasures to be from His hand.

So let's not go around compartmentalizing—editing, cutting, pasting, filing, and sorting away our life experiences into that which is neatly spiritual and neatly secular. As a believer, you can make every area of life sacred.

The Bible says *whatever* we do—whether we eat fresh asparagus, listen to Beethoven, play Pictionary, hug our spouse, or tackle a challenging ski slope—can and should be glorifying to God.

That's such an encouraging thought I can't wait to plug it into my computer—umm, I mean, life.

FULL MOON

There's going to be a full moon tonight in a soft, clear, Southern California sky. And I'm going to be outside enjoying it.

Does that make me sound like a romantic? Well, maybe. But I just love the silvery sheen of a bright, moonlit night. The shadows are long, and common shapes and figures take on an almost magical quality. Maybe Ken and I will go for a walk in the moonlit neighborhood.

That's what our family used to do back on the farm in Maryland. Sometimes we would even saddle up our horses and go for a moonlight ride. What fun! Laughter in the night. The clip-clop of horse hooves. Pale light turning the gravel road into a silver ribbon. Funny, romantic songs about the moon.

To me as a child, it was all so wonderful.

On one of those moonlight rides, I remember my father telling us about the relationship between the moon and the sun. He explained how the sun—in all its glory and greatness—was the source of our world's light. And though the sun was on the other side of the earth and out of sight, the moon, devoid of any brightness of its own, reflected the light of the sun. Like a mirror, the moon was in the right place at the right time—the best position to reflect the brightness of the sun.

Daddy went on to tell us that we as Christians relate to our Lord much like the moon relates to the sun. If we're lined up in His will, we are in the best position to reflect the glory of the Son, Jesus Christ. For that matter, like the moon, we can only *reflect* His light. We have no real goodness, no real virtue, apart from our Lord. He is the Source of it all and the best we can do is get in a right relationship to Him so that we can be His light here on earth.

In John 9:5 Jesus said, "While I am in the world, I am the light of the world." And then He reminds us in Matthew 5 that *we* are the light of the world. "Let your light shine before men," He tells us, "that they may see your good deeds and praise your Father in heaven" (vv. 14, 16).

So, if you happen to step outside tonight on this full moonlit evening, let that shining orb call you back to your purpose on this old planet. Get in the right position. Get in right relationship with God. Reflect the light and love of the Sun of Righteousness (Malachi 4:2).

PILGRIM OR TOURIST?

When I was growing up, we used to visit my Uncle Ted's ranch in Tie Siding, Wyoming.

What an adventure! It was a real working cattle ranch with plenty of chores for young Maryland cowgirls. My sisters and I even had a part in branding some of the calves.

Uncle Ted put me on a big old retired workhorse and it was my job to keep the cows corralled at one end of the arena while at the other end the cowboys would use their cutting horses to single out calves for branding. Even though my horse and I just stood there most of the time, watching all the action across the way, I still felt as though I had a special job minding those cows.

Because my Uncle Ted's ranch was situated near Laramie, tourists would often come by to take a look at what a real cattle ranch was all about. They would stand at a polite distance, casually observing all the goings on, occasionally pointing, or pulling out their cameras.

I was just a little tyke then, but I can remember straightening my cowboy hat and sitting up in my saddle to pose for snapshots—as though I was a permanent fixture around the place. It never occurred to me back then that I was just passing through like those tourists—that I was only going to be at the ranch a short time.

Yet even though Uncle Ted's was not my permanent place of residence, I got a lot more involved than the average tourist. For a short time at least, I was part of a working ranch.

It's been years since I've visited Tie Siding. But to this day I've resisted the label of "tourist." Whenever I visit places around the world, I'm not satisfied to stand at a distance snapping pictures. I like to get involved. To do things. To talk with people who live in the area. To learn about customs. I don't want to be considered a tourist with funny clothes and a Kodak. I want to be part of things.

As a Christian living out the kingdom of God down here on earth, I feel the same way. True, the Bible tells us we are to be pilgrims on this planet. That is, we must not mistake this world for home.

But I don't think Scripture encourages us to be mere "tourists" either—casually observing all the goings-on around at a polite, safe distance. "You are the salt of the earth," Jesus told us in Matthew 5. "You are the light of the world." God wants us to get involved, to rub shoulders with folks around us, even though we're only going to be here for a season. We've got work to do here—and only a short time to do it.

Do you consider yourself a pilgrim when it comes to living out the life of Christ? Or are you more like a tourist, staying at arm's-length from any kind of serious involvement in your church, neighborhood, and community?

There are too many tourists crowding their way through life already. God doesn't want any more spectators. He needs pilgrims, sober-minded and serious, who will make their impact for Him on their way through this life and into the next.

So put your camera away and climb on a horse, pardner. There's room in the corral for you.

RECONNECTING

Have you ever attempted a spiritual task under your own steam?

There have been more than a couple of times when I have either given my testimony, or spoken on some topic from the Bible, fully aware that I was doing so apart from the power of God.

On those occasions I have sounded absolutely hollow. More than that, I have *felt* hollow. Even though sharing powerful truths from God's Word, I knew that *my* words lacked any power whatsoever.

It's strange when that happens. It's an odd feeling of being separated from myself somehow . . . like something is disconnected. Sometimes, right in the middle of what I'm saying, I will breathe a silent prayer of repentance. From that point on, I can easily tell the difference between my efforts and God's energy working through me.

David speaks truly in Psalm 22:29: "None can keep alive his own soul" (KJV). What a mechanical thing life becomes when we attempt to live a supernatural life apart from supernatural power. Prayer becomes dull. Relationships sag under the weight of selfishness. Our jobs seem like robotic routine. Witnessing becomes an unpleasant duty. Doing some act of kindness feels like a tiresome chore. When we try to "keep alive our own soul," we fail miserably.

Could it be that life has seemed so smooth for you lately because you've been feeling a little self-sufficient? Maybe you've conquered a certain temptation by the grace of God, and you'd like very much to pat yourself on the back. "You'll never catch me doing *that* again!" you tell yourself.

Or perhaps you catch yourself thinking, "Well, I understand how business operates, and there's no need to wait upon God for direction in so simple a matter."

Hear again the words of the psalmist: *"None can keep alive his own soul."*

Consider the plea of the apostle: *"Count yourselves dead to sin but alive to God in Christ Jesus. . . . Just as Christ was raised from the dead through the glory of the Father, we too may live a new life"* (Romans 6:11, 4).

We wouldn't think of pushing our car up and down the freeway whenever we wanted to go somewhere—not when all that power is available to us at the turn of a key. It's just as absurd to think we can live our Christian lives apart from the hour-by-hour, moment-by-moment empowering of our Lord Jesus.

QUALITY AND QUANTITY

Have you ever wondered why Jesus launched His public ministry by turning water into wine at a wedding party?

Just last night I puzzled over that question as I read the second chapter of John. Why that particular miracle at that particular time? And why wine?

I once heard my friend, Bible teacher Kay Arthur, describe that miracle as one of the highest *quality and quantity*. "That," she exclaimed, "is the way Jesus does things!"

Let's think about that. Those six stone jars Jesus told the servants to fill with water were huge. Each container held up to *thirty gallons.* Have you ever tried to lift or carry thirty gallons of anything? And those servants, Scripture tells us, filled each jar "to the brim." It must have been tough hauling those enormous jugs from the well into the house.

When Jesus changed that plain Galilean water into chablis—or whatever it was—the wedding party ended up with 180 gallons of it! That, my friends, is a lot of wine. There's no way folks at that wedding would be able to drink that much, that fast. It was far more than they needed. Surely, one thirty-gallon jar would have been plenty. Hadn't the guests already consumed every drop of wine in the house?

But that's what Jesus chose to do. He gave much more than anyone would have expected.

And then there was the quality of that wine. This wasn't "California Cooler." It wasn't plain label jug stuff. It was strictly gold medallion—probably ten grades above the best contemporary French vintage. The quality of that miraculous wine was absolute tops.

The master of the banquet was incredulous after he tasted the fresh supply. "Why in the world did you save the best for last?" he asked the bridegroom. "You could have gotten by with a bargain brand at this point in the feast!"

But that's what Jesus chose to do. He gave much better than anyone would have expected.

It was as Kay Arthur said: a miracle of quality and quantity. And that's what He wants to do in your life today. He says to you as He said to His disciples long ago: "I have come that [you] may have life, and have it to the full" (John 10:10). The life He's talking about, of course, is *His* life, flowing in and through you.

When it comes to *quantity*, this is life that bubbles up and spills over the rim. More than you ever expected or could possibly contain.

When it comes to *quality*, this is the very life of God. We are, as Peter says, "participators in the divine nature." It is the best life that can be.

The key? Well, let's give some credit to Mary, the Lord's mother. The counsel she gave to those servants that day at the wedding can hardly be improved upon:

"Do whatever he tells you" (John 2:5).

Submit to His Lordship, do exactly as He says . . . and be prepared for a life full of surprises.

STILL LIFE?

As an artist, I've always been challenged by still life.

Contrary to what you might think, still life has to be more than a collection of objects occupying space on a table. Those images must compel the viewer to become involved. They must unlock memories, evoke mental images. While the painting itself doesn't move, it must move something within one who views.

No, a bowl of fruit doesn't jump around, but it *does* have life. The challenge is to make a banana look like it's begging to be peeled. Dying to get eaten.

When I paint a bell, I want that bell to do what it was made to do. A painted bell that doesn't *ring* in the viewer's mind is a dead thing. Something less than a bell.

If I paint a candle I want the viewer to smell the fragrance of melting wax and feel the heat of the flame.

Fruit. Bells. Candles. These must be more than lifeless ornaments. They must perform their appointed tasks in the imagination of the one who stands before the painting. Why? Because that is what we expect of their real-life counterparts. A piece of fruit that sits undisturbed and uneaten in a bowl will soon rot—unless it's made of wax. An ornamental candle that languishes for years in a brass holder never fulfills its destiny. A voiceless bell that collects dust on somebody's knickknack shelf is a mockery to its creator.

As I consider these thoughts, it comes to me that some of us Christians have become "still life." We give every appearance of pious, church-going, Bible-believing disciples of Jesus. But we're still life—and we know it. A one-dimensional painting. An ornament on display. A knickknack on the shelf. Nice to look at and be looked up to . . . but rarely put to good use. Down in our hearts, we know we're gathering dust, letting the years slip by, not really doing and being what God intended us to do and be.

The book of James offers succinct counsel for ornamental Christians. "Do not merely listen to the word, and so deceive yourselves," the apostle writes. *"Do what it says"* (James 1:22).

Just as bells are meant to ring, you and I are meant to sound out the good news of Jesus.

Just as candles are meant to burn, you and I are meant to stir the fires of the Spirit within us.

Just as fruit is meant to nourish and refresh, you and I are meant to bear the fragrant, life-giving fruit of the Spirit of Christ for the sake of hungry, discouraged men and women.

Life, you see, is never really still.

Only death is still.

"LORD, MAKE ME USABLE"

"Lord, please use me!"

It's the cry of believers who want to salt their world with the words and life of Jesus. Their heart's desire may not be unlike that old hymn:

Have Thine own way, Lord, have Thine own way!
Thou art the potter, I am the clay.
Mold me and make me, after Thy will,
while I am waiting, yielded and still.

Do you want to be used by the Lord? Good news! God *wants* to use you. In fact, He *will* use you. In John 15:8 Jesus says it is to His Father's glory that we bear much fruit, showing ourselves to be disciples. In other words, it is His will to use us.

Frankly, I think we're being redundant to ask God to use us. We're requesting Him to do something He already desires to do.

So maybe we should amend that prayer. Instead of praying, "Lord, use me," perhaps our prayer should be, "Lord, make me *usable.*"

Do you catch the difference?

If we feel like we're sitting on the sidelines, watching the army of Christ go marching by, we mustn't pray to be used; rather, we must plead with the Lord to make our lives usable and useful.

"Mold me and make me after Thy will," says the hymn. "While I am waiting, *yielded* and still."

That implies reflection, doesn't it? And humility. And Spirit-guided self-examination.

Ponder Paul's familiar words to his young colleague:

In a large house there are articles not only of gold and silver, but also of wood and clay; some are for noble purposes and some for ignoble. If a man cleanses himself from the latter, he will be an instrument for noble purposes, made holy, useful to the Master and prepared to do any good work (2 Timothy 2:20-21).

234

Seems to me as I read those words that the responsibility for usefulness doesn't fall so much on the Master of the household who chooses instruments, as on the instrument itself. If a man or woman is clean and ready to be used, he or she *will be* "useful to the Master and prepared to do any good work."

And how does that instrument prepare itself for noble service? Paul immediately goes on to lay down some specifics:

> Flee the evil desires of youth, and pursue righteousness, faith, love and peace, along with those who call on the Lord out of a pure heart. Don't have anything to do with foolish and stupid arguments, because you know they produce quarrels. And the Lord's servant must not quarrel; instead, he must be kind to everyone, able to teach, not resentful (vv. 22-24).

Perhaps we ought to spend a little less time chomping on the bit.

Sure, you may have a talent for singing . . . but God may be more concerned with getting your heart and character in tune.

Yes, you may be a gifted teacher . . . but perhaps God has a few inside lessons to teach you before you go out and lead others.

True, you may be anxious to plunge into full-time service for your Lord . . . but it might pay to see if your own house is in order first.

Instead of the old "Lord-use-me" prayer, you might try praying something different for a change.

> *Lord, I already know You want to use me. I don't have to ask You to do that. You want my life to be a ready instrument for your purposes here on earth. Please show me those things that keep me from being that instrument. Show me those areas of my life that slow Your hand when You reach for a ready tool. I wait before You, Lord . . . yielded and still.*

ASSURANCE

*God's Personal Involvement
in My Life*

10

ASSURANCE
God's Personal Involvement
in My Life

It's a question that nags every little boy or girl at some point. *What if I did something REALLY bad and Mom and Dad decided to disown me?*

I toyed with such scary thoughts when I was a child. Especially when I'd misbehaved. Like the time my Uncle Dick caught me smoking a cigarette behind his old Studebaker parked in my grandmother's driveway. I just knew if he told Mom I would end up in that German orphanage at the end of Monastery Avenue.

239

Oddly, I can't recall the punishment my parents gave me. But I wasn't sent to any orphanage. And sometime afterwards, in a more confident moment, I confided to Mother those worst fears. She just laughed in an understanding way and hugged me close.

Not long ago I talked to a man whose parents actually disowned him. Don recounted how he had formerly been a Benedictine monk, the pride of his Italian family. As a monk, he lived behind ivy-covered walls. For a time he settled into the routine . . . morning prayers, humble work in a small garden.

But then, through a series of improbable circumstances, he came to faith in Christ and left the monastery. His family was mortified. And then when Christ led Don to make some tough, uncompromising decisions, his parents simply washed their hands of him. His father disowned him, wrote him out of the will, and went so far as to actually mourn his son's "death."

Can you imagine the pain Don felt?

After that conversation with Don, I couldn't help but recall a curious fact a lawyer friend told me years ago. While a father can disown his natural-born offspring, the lawyer told me, he *cannot* disown an adopted son or daughter.

I don't pretend to understand all the legal reasoning behind that statute, but it has been a traditional law in culture after culture since the time of Christ.

Could the apostle Paul have had this legality in mind when he penned his letter to the Galatians? I wonder. When God sent forth His Son, he wrote, it was to "redeem those who were under the Law, that we might receive the adoption as sons . . . Therefore you are no longer a slave, but a son; and if a son, then an heir through God" (4: 5, 7 NASB).

Keeping that adoption rule in mind, it could have been Paul's way of underlining a critical truth: As adopted children of our heavenly Father, we will *never* be disowned. Not in time. Not in eternity. Again, in Romans 8 the apostle wrote:

> You have received a spirit of adoption as sons by which we cry out, "Abba! Father!" The Spirit Himself bears witness with our spirit that we are children of

God, and if children, heirs also, heirs of God and fellow heirs with Christ (vv. 15-17, NASB).

Sometimes, like a worried little child, you may be tempted to fear God will disown you for one reason or another. Perhaps you imagine Him saying, "If you don't stop acting like a little rebel, I'm going to leave you. No more intrusions into *your* life! I'm going to write you out of the will."

Bring those foolish worries to God and let Him soothe your doubts away. Grip the reality of His eternal Word, and don't let go. God will never disown you. He will never write you out of His will. He will never leave you or cease to be a Glorious Intruder in your life. What He has given Christ, His first and only Son, He will freely give *you* as an adopted son or daughter.

My friend Don draws comfort from that thought. So do I. And it's my earnest hope that as you read the following pages, you too will rest in the certainty that God, the Glorious Intruder, will forever hold you close as His much-loved child. God wants you to be assured of His love!

So continue to stand on Scripture. Grow in Him. *And rest assured!*

WORTH YOUR WEIGHT IN WEAKNESS

I remember the time my sister Jay and I took old Route 40 from the farm down to an auction at the Baltimore Livestock Exchange.

We'd heard a nearby thoroughbred farm was relinquishing stock, and thought we might be able to pick up a good horse—cheap.

Arriving early, we walked around the pens to examine the animals up for bid. I had my eye on a huge red thoroughbred nobody else seemed to be looking at—but we didn't want to appear too anxious in front of the seller.

Trying my best to look cool and professional, I ran my hand down the horse's shins, feeling for any bumps to indicate shin splints. I knelt and ran my fingers over his hooves, looking for any cracks or splits. We rubbed his ribs, felt his withers, looked at his teeth, lifted his tail . . . and finally stepped back to assess his general condition.

By the time we were through with that thoroughbred, we knew all his weak spots. And we knew exactly what he was worth. We were more than ready to point out those weaknesses to the owner if he didn't want to accept our low bid.

Weak spots. It's scary to think of having your weak spots exposed, isn't it? Weaknesses have a way of either raising or lowering our value in the eyes of others.

I'm reminded of a quote by Corrie ten Boom.

> The devil is like a good cattle dealer who walks once around a cow and then knows all its weak spots. He knows us and knows exactly where he can hit us. The devil has not yet retired. He knows that his time is short and he's extremely active. But Jesus is present, much stronger than the devil.

Fair warning. You may think you've got your weaknesses covered, but your Enemy would like to get the lowest possible bid on your life. To do so, he'll make certain he's looked you over, up and down, left and right, this way and that.

Satan is *very* interested in your weak spots. Whether it's a tendency to fear, a propensity to doubt, a pull toward fantasizing, or a leaning toward pride, he's got your number.

If you sense an area of intense struggle in your life right now, you'd best realize the devil will continue to pressure you where it hurts. He knows your down-side, and isn't a bit reluctant to make full use of that knowledge.

But like Corrie said, Jesus is ever-so present, and much stronger than the devil. He also knows your weak spots, but He wants those vulnerable areas to become His power points in your life. Realizing this, Paul was able to write: "When I am weak, *then* I am strong" (2 Corinthians 12:10).

In spite of all your failings and struggles, the Lord Jesus did not purchase your life at low bid. No higher price could have been paid.

From His point of view, you're worth your weight in weaknesses.

His First Sermon

For we do not have a high priest who is unable to sympa-thize with our weaknesses, but we have one who has been tempted in every way, just as we are—yet was without sin (Hebrews 4:15).

When we think of the trials and temptations of the God-Man, we usually think of His wilderness experience. His desperate hunger and fiery thirst. Or that darkest of hours when His friends abandoned Him. We remember He had no place to call home. We recall He walked hundreds of weary miles. His muscles ached and His feet blistered. He cried real tears. And when they pinioned His body to that rough wooden cross, He not only bore our sins, but He *became* sin for us. He identified with every area of our human weakness.

But that profound identification didn't start with His public ministry. No. When I think of the extent Christ went to probe the depths of human experience, I think of His birth.

Even as a baby, He identified. No pastel-papered, hygienic nursery for Him. No brand-new crib and changing table. No disposable diapers and baby powder. No musical mobiles of giraffes and Teddy bears. No cotton swabs and baby ointment. No pink and blue needlepoint hanging on the wall. And His swaddling clothes were a far cry from Carter's top-of-the-line.

Right from the beginning of His journey on earth, the Lord Jesus sympathized with our weaknesses. He entered history in a smelly stable with a handful of hay for a pillow. The only music He heard may have been the muffled strains of a lyre and flute from the crowded inn nearby. The first fragrance to fill his nostrils was musty straw and animal manure. His first bed was a feed trough. His first changing table was a dirt floor.

Not one of us can ever point an accusing finger at Jesus and say, "You live in an ivory tower . . . You don't know what it's like!"

Maybe God planned it that way to make a point. Perhaps our heavenly Father wanted us to understand that in weakness there is strength. In poverty, riches. In humiliation, dignity.

Even as a baby, the Lord Jesus had a mission. Before He could even speak, His life was a message. His birth, in many ways, was a sermon. From the very beginning He was demonstrating the extent to which divine love would reach.

This is the High Priest to whom we give our praises—during the Christmas season and all year long. This is the One we adore and to whom we sing our thanksgivings. We have a Savior who sympathizes with our weaknesses.

"Let us then approach the throne of grace with confidence" (Hebrews 4:16).

Because Jesus knows.

Because Jesus understands.

History and heaven defy anyone to say otherwise.

WHY?

I'm glad I'm not an Old Testament saint. I don't think I could wait as long as many of them did to get answers to their pain-filled questions.

Take Gideon, for example.

One day as he went about his work hidden in a winepress, the angel of the Lord appeared to him and called out, "The LORD is with you, mighty warrior." Gideon looked around at his surroundings, and what he saw didn't match the angel's greeting. *If I'm such a mighty warrior,* he must have thought, *then why am I secretly threshing wheat in the middle of a winepress?"* The angelic statement deserved a pointed question, and Gideon asked it:

> If the LORD is with us, why has all this happened to us? Where are all his wonders that our fathers told us about when they said, "Did not the LORD bring us up out of Egypt?" But now the LORD has abandoned us and put us into the hand of Midian.

Well, the Lord hadn't abandoned them, and the story turns out happily; but Gideon never did get his questions answered.

Or take another example. Immediately after praising God's great acts of redemption and proclaiming his undying confidence in God's care, the writer of Psalm 44 says:

> But now you have rejected and humbled us; you no longer go out with our armies. You made us retreat before the enemy, and our adversaries have plundered us . . . You sold your people for a pittance, gaining nothing from their sale . . . All this happened to us, though we had not forgotten you or been false to your covenant. Our hearts had not turned back; our feet had not strayed from your path. But you crushed us and made us a haunt for jackals and covered us over with deep darkness . . . Yet for your sake we face death all day long; we are considered as sheep to be slaughtered (vv. 9-10, 12, 17-19, 22).

And then comes his question:

> Why do you hide your face and forget our misery and oppression? (v. 24).

A hard question. A painful question. A question God never answers . . . until you get to the New Testament.

"Why do you hide your face and forget our misery and oppression?"—have you ever felt like that? Has it ever seemed that God has abandoned you even though you've remained faithful to Him? Has unexpected pain or calamity or sickness or tragedy or misfortune come storming into your life, leaving you bleeding and mumbling, "Why?"

I've been there, too, friend. So has Gideon. So has the writer of Psalm 44. But what those men didn't have, and we do, is found snuggled up in Paul's amazing promise in Romans 8. That's where you'll find God's answer to their agonized "Whys?"

When we understand at least a few of the whys, we have the confidence that we're not simply suffering for nothing. And the best reason I can think of for my own paralysis is Romans 8:28. It says there that "All things fit together in a pattern for good, to them that love God, for the purpose of conforming you to the image of Jesus Christ" (personal translation).

Now, before my injury when I was a young teenager on my feet, I cared very little about being made more like Christ. The greatest amount of suffering I ever went through was sweating out twenty-five laps on the hockey field or failing a chemistry quiz, or perhaps feeling shunned by a couple of classmates in some clique.

Suffering seemed to have little connection with the abundant Christian life. I thought the abundant life meant less homework, more popularity, and good grades. Being made more like Christ was something to worry about when I got older.

My ideas took a sharp turn after my injury at the age of seventeen. Suddenly I began to see that suffering really was inextricably linked with being made more like Christ. Helplessness really had something to do with holiness, and pain had a great deal to do with piety. My value system began to change. The abundant Christian life now meant any degree of Christ's character that could be found in me—like peace or patience, endurance, tolerance, kindness, sensitivity. It dawned on me that this is what real success and beauty was all about—Jesus living in, and reflecting through, me.

Now, don't think I'm glorifying suffering. There is nothing intrinsically good about being paralyzed. There is nothing inherently good about blindness or deafness. There is nothing innately good about war or violence or deformities or divorce, bankruptcy or poverty. But these things—bad as they are—can fit into a marvelous plan for our good and His glory.

Remember the psalmist's question? Here it is again: "Why do you hide your face and forget our misery and oppression?" Who wouldn't have a hard time being assured of God's unwavering love when, for His sake, "we face death all day long; we are considered as sheep to be slaughtered"?

Yet, amazing as it seems, it's this very phrase about suffering sheep that Paul picks up in Romans 8:36 to proclaim God's love. Look it up for yourself. Even in the midst of pain, Paul says, even when our lives hang by a thread, it is in those very times that "we are more than conquerors through him who loved us. For I am convinced that neither death nor life, neither angels nor demons, neither the present nor the future, nor any powers, neither height nor depth, nor anything else in all creation, will be able to separate us from the love of God" (vv. 37-39).

Right now, put *your* problems on that list. Even these things, great or small, the things you're struggling with, cannot separate you from the love of God. And the extra plus is that through it all Jesus is being ingrained in your character.

And that's an answer you can live with.

THE OTHER KIND OF SUFFERING

Her name is Kerrie, the thirteen-year-old daughter of one of the women I work with in the office. Occasionally Kerrie volunteers after school at her mother's side, stuffing envelopes, photocopying resource lists, and sorting brochures. She's a shy little girl who spends a lot of time alone, reading, drawing, and doing puzzles.

There's a deeper reason why Kerrie is so shy, so withdrawn.

Junior high hasn't been easy for her. She's the one who's left out in the cafeteria. She's the one who walks down the hall alone. She's the target of the name-callers. She's the one who's had to brush dried food out of her hair—food thrown by hateful classmates.

I look at her, bewildered. I simply don't understand. Kerrie is a kind, sensitive girl, a smattering of pale freckles across cheeks that apple-up when she smiles. She offers no retort to her tormentors, no resistance, no angry backbiting. I haven't yet figured out why the boys and girls in her school treat her so spitefully. What makes it so cruel is the anguish this girl suffers. Deep pain and perplexity, smothered and suppressed, still shows in her eyes.

Does our Lord identify with that kind of suffering?

We all know Christ suffered. We immediately picture the crown of thorns the soldier ground into His scalp, or the nails thrust through His hands and feet. The cross, understandably, is synonymous with the suffering of Christ.

But sometimes it's hard to identify with that kind of pain. Yes, He suffered unbearably during those dark hours but . . . that's not the sort of suffering most of us have to face. Like my young friend Kerrie our suffering is often on the *inside*. Out of sight. Bloodless. Silent. Hidden from others.

We often suffer intense relational pain—the hurts, slights, rejections, and put-downs inflicted by others. No, it isn't a scourging or a beating. There aren't any literal nails or thorns. But it still hurts. Sometimes unbearably so.

Can we be certain our Lord identifies with *that* sort of non-spectacular, "everyday" pain?

Isaiah 53 must lay any such doubt to rest. In verse after verse the prophet paints a profoundly personal portrait of the Messiah. Within those lines—and often between the lines—we catch a glimpse of the everyday pain Jesus Christ endured as He walked on the earth.

Early in the chapter we learn that Jesus was not necessarily the most attractive guy on earth.

> He had no beauty or majesty to attract us to him,
> nothing in his appearance that we should desire him.
> He was despised and rejected by men, a man of sorrows, and familiar with suffering (vv. 2-3).

There was nothing about His looks that particularly drew people. He was just your everyday, ordinary-looking, Jewish young man.

There are plenty of plain Janes and John Does who can identify with Isaiah 53:2. I've had those days too—days when you look in the mirror and feel downright unattractive. Even ugly. But the Bible tells us we have a Savior who knows what that sort of rejection and loneliness is all about.

Verse 6 reveals even more.

> We all, like sheep, have gone astray,
>> each of us has turned to his own way;
> and the LORD has laid on him
>> the iniquity of us all.

Everybody turned away from Him. Alone, Jesus shouldered the burden of our sin and rebellion. Just as you have felt the stab of other people's pity or the indifference of uncaring friends, Jesus, too, endured the sting of rebuff and the ache of loneliness. And it wasn't an occasional thing from a few fair-weather friends. He felt the awful realization that *no one* was on His side. No one bothered to listen or care.

Verse 11 speaks of the "suffering of his soul." That has to be the worst kind of suffering possible . . . when you cry those deep, heaving sobs that come from *way* down inside. Real anguish you just can't stop.

You know how that feels. So does He.

So if you're experiencing relational pain today, battling with that ache that goes right through you, remember that your High Priest perfectly understands.

Yes, His suffering went far beyond what you and I will ever understand—all the way to the cross. But He also understands how it feels to be ignored, spurned, and devalued.

If you bring that pain to Him, He will never make light of it.

COMFORTER

A very special grandmother recently told me of an experience with her young granddaughter . . . and a Glorious Intruder.

My daughter's call from the hospital emergency room shocked me. My granddaughter Robin, just turned six, had fallen from the high bar at school, severely injuring her mouth. I picked up her sisters from school and spent a hectic, tense afternoon supervising the little ones while awaiting my daughter's return with Robin.

The doctor had taken eight stitches inside her mouth and six on the outside. As the little ones swarmed over their mother, Robin sat squarely in the biggest chair in the living room. Her face puffed almost beyond recognition, her long hair still ropey with dried blood, she looked tiny and forlorn. Still, I approached her cautiously, for Robin is the least demonstrative, most private of children.

"Is there anything you want, darling?" I asked.

She looked me firmly in the eye and said, "I want a hug."

Me too! I thought as I cuddled her on my lap. *But how and whom does an exhausted grandmother ask?* As we rocked gently, the words of Scripture came from John 14:16: "I will pray the Father, and He shall give you another Comforter, that He may abide with you for ever."

So I asked, just as simply and plaintively as Robin had asked. And just as simply, I felt His everlasting arms enfold us.

Like that grandmother, we often long to have comforting arms surround us in our weariness, heartache, and confusion.

That's what I love about the Holy Spirit.

Certainly, the Bible names Him as our Counselor. And yes, He is our Intercessor. We're told elsewhere He is our Teacher, Guide, and the Spirit of Truth. He reminds us of everything Jesus has said. He reveals the Father. He even convicts us of sin. He does so many things. But one thing I love most . . .

He's our Comforter.

There are times when I so yearn to feel the presence of God I almost weep. And I know it is at those times the Holy Spirit is earnestly praying for me. What a comfort to sense His presence in such a close and personal way!

The Lord Jesus tells us in John 16:14 that the Holy Spirit will only bring glory to Him. How true that is. When I sense the consoling presence of the Spirit, it makes me want to praise Jesus all the more.

If you're hurting today, don't immediately grab the phone to call a friend. Seek the everlasting arms of the Spirit. He is many things, but most importantly to you today, He is your Comforter. He has a ready embrace for hurting little girls, heartsick grandmas, worried daddies . . . and you, too, by the way.

You say it's been a while since you've sensed that holy hug?

Maybe it's been a while since you've asked.

GOD PURSUES US

When I stumbled headlong into my first big trial as a new Christian, I wondered just where the love of God had gone.

People spoke of God's love helping me through hard times, yet I couldn't shake a mental image of Him leaning against some ivory wall in heaven, casually thumbing in the direction of the cross. "That says it all," I imagined Him saying.

I soon discovered I wasn't alone in that attitude. I've talked to a number of people over the years who imagine a bored, lethargic God . . . a God only passively interested in our circumstances—and slightly irritated if pushed to demonstrate His present-day love. Some describe Him as little more than a cosmic Warehouse Clerk, filling mail-order prayer requests. Others feel God abandons them when some other, "more obedient" Christian catches His attention.

My perception of Him has changed, of course, as I've grown in my faith. But even those of us who view Him as a powerful, caring God easily underestimate the strength of His determined love.

God does not observe our lives at a cool distance. He is neither apathetic nor detached. He is on the move. He is involved.

Listen to Andrew Greeley . . .

Our God is not patiently standing by and waiting for us to offer love; He is actively and vigorously pursuing us . . . He is the father running down the trail to embrace the prodigal son even before the boy can speak his act of contrition. He is the mad farmer showering a full day's wage on men who hadn't even worked. He is Jesus forgiving the sinful woman even before she spoke her sorrow. He is the king lavishing a banquet on beggars. These are all symbols of a God whose love for us is so active, so strong, that by human standards He would be, at least, said to be mad.

God is not the sort to casually murmur, "Well, sure I love you." He constantly shows how much.

Consider the impact we would have on our world if we began to pursue God with some of the intensity with which He seeks us! If we would respond in obedience the instant we discerned the Spirit's prodding. If we, like God, had a passion for holiness. If we would freely pour out our love as He does.

In a day when it's fashionable to appear cool, bored, uncaring, and detached, we can't afford to doubt the enthusiastic, all-encompassing love of God. His compelling love surrounds us every minute. He's in front of us, behind us, relentlessly pouring His love into our lives. What madness! What a passion for our souls! How can we be halfhearted toward our circumstances—toward others—when He loves us so?

May we be found running down the trail to forgive those who offend us.

May we shower our abundance on those who don't deserve it.

May we embrace the sinner before he even speaks his sorrow.

And may we pursue our God with even a fraction of the energy with which He pursues us.

WHERE THE WIND BLOWS

The Carpenter must have paused in the conversation, feeling a cool evening wind touch His face, tug at His robe. He may have gestured toward the dark shape of a nearby tree, listening to a murmur of leaves.

"The wind," He told the Pharisee, "blows wherever it pleases. You hear its sound, but you cannot tell where it comes from or where it is going. So it is with everyone born of the Spirit" (John 3:8).

I've always loved that illustration.

Maybe it's because I've always loved the wind.

I think of a summer afternoon . . . relaxing underneath an old, wide-armed maple, watching the wind gently bend the branches and rustle the leaves.

I think of a morning by the ocean . . . feeling the wind in my face, watching it toss the waves.

I think of camping in a grove of pine . . . listening to the wind whistle and whisper through the forest.

I think of a November nor'easter . . . roaring across rain-wet fields in wild and wonderful fury.

I think of the smell of wind . . . bearing the fragrance of distant blossoms, the aroma of a cherrywood fire, the sharp, salt-tang of the sea.

Little wonder Jesus likened the wind to the Spirit. Wind, by its very nature, *moves*. Just so, the Spirit never lies dormant, never stays still within the soul. He's always moving, always making His presence known. And if this Holy One truly lives at the center of our lives, we will see . . . feel . . . at times almost smell and hear the effects of His activity. The Spirit will constantly be *doing* something within us, something others will be able to observe.

Although we cannot see the wind with our eyes, we know it moves among us by the effect it has on trees, flowers, ocean waves, smoke from fires, ripples on a pond, waving wheat, and its touch on our faces.

In the same way, you will know the Spirit lives in you or a fellow Christian by the effect He produces in character and conduct.

It's absurd to suppose you can have the Spirit of Christ within you and *not* see, feel, and experience His presence. The Holy Spirit *will* produce holy living. Paul says in Galatians 5:22 that "the fruit [or evidence] of the Spirit is love, joy, peace, patience, kindness, goodness, faithfulness, gentleness and self-control."

The wind marks its movement by what it touches. And in its wake it leaves freshness and cleansing.

As you allow the Spirit to fill and empower your life, others will mark His presence, breathe deeply of His fragrance . . . and give thanks.

THE MASTER'S TOUCH

He began his career as a jockey—a wiry, short, but very strong boy from Italy.

It didn't take him long to make a name for himself around the stables and among the top owners. After jockeying a number of blue-ribbon thoroughbreds, he went on to become a master horse trainer. You could ask most anybody around Baltimore's Pimlico race track back in the 1940s. Pop Trombero was one of the best.

By the time I met Pop in the mid 1960s, he had long since retired from the track. Actually, Pop became family . . . my sister's father-in-law. At various family gatherings Pop would come to our farm and go horseback riding with us.

On one such occasion I recall my sister asking me to let Pop ride my horse, Tumbleweed. I protested. Listen, that horse was *mine*, and I didn't want anyone else riding her—even if he was an "expert."

After a few minutes, however, I felt ashamed and gave in. I watched Pop Trombero tighten his jockey saddle on Tumbleweed as I saddled one of the older, slower horses. While we rode, I stuck close to Pop and Tumbleweed—just to make sure he didn't jerk on her bridle or tug at her reins.

After a few minutes together on the trail, I realized I had nothing to worry about. In fact, observing the way Pop handled my horse, I grudgingly realized I had a few things to learn. He was so . . . *tender* with Tumbleweed. Constantly talking to her. Continually stroking her neck. Always giving her his undivided attention. No matter how interesting the trail, Pop's focus never diverted from that horse for a moment.

You wouldn't believe the way Tumbleweed responded. She became a different horse! Her ears pricked up. She listened to his commands, never balked, obeyed instantly. It seemed her joy to do Pop's bidding. I was amazed! I looked down at my mount, realizing I'd hardly paid any attention to the animal. And the way my horse acted, it showed.

Wonderful things happened when a master like Pop touched a horse. He knew how to guide. He knew how to bring out the best.

And wonderful things happen when the Master touches our lives as well. Mark 6:56 tells us that ". . . as many as touched Him were made whole" (KJV).

His attention never diverts from you for a moment. His touch in your life is constant, unchanging, always tender.

Is it the joy of your heart to do His will? To obey? To pick up your pace when you feel His nudge? To slow down at a gentle tug on the reins?

The Lord God knows how to guide you as no one else. He knows how to bring out your best.

It's a matter of yielding to the Master's touch.

THE DETAILS COUNT

God's greatest plans often seem to rest on the tiniest of details.

Take something as critical and foundational as the selection and anointing of David as king of Israel. The prophet Samuel visits Jesse's house on a prospecting tour of his sons.

> Jesse had seven of his sons pass before Samuel, but Samuel said to him, "The LORD has not chosen these." So he asked Jesse, "Are these all the sons you have?" (1 Samuel 16:10-11).

What if Samuel had *not* asked that question?

What if he had simply shrugged his shoulders and chose one of the other sons of Jesse to be king of Israel? The whole future of the Jewish race hung in the balance with that one tiny question. From our perspective at least, the lineage of Christ Himself depended on one little, seemingly insignificant query.

But Samuel *did* ask the question. "These fellows are just fine, Jesse, fine specimens of manhood. But . . . don't you have any more?"

With that little question, history remained on course.

Look at the story of Esther. The entire Jewish race was about to be exterminated under the reign of Persian King Xerxes. But in Esther 6:1, we read: "That night the king could not sleep; so he ordered the book of the chronicles, the record of his reign, to be brought in and read to him." From there, the story goes on to report that the king found a very special Jew highlighted in the chronicles. The king decided to honor Esther's uncle, thereby saving an entire race . . . and more.

But what if the king, on that fateful night when he could not sleep, had asked for a Sidney Sheldon novel? What if he had decided not to read, but to raid the royal icebox? What if he had opted for entertainment by the court jester? What if he'd popped a Sominex or two?

There are a million what-ifs. But the king—in God's sovereign plan—chose instead to read the chronicles . . . something like back issues of *U. S. News & World Report.* And there was that little item about Esther's uncle that jumped right off the scroll at him.

It overwhelms me to think about details. Small things. Small happenings. Truly, the greatest plans of God often hinge on the tiniest occurrences.

Do you ever find yourself tempted to think God isn't concerned with the details of your life? Do you ever find yourself imagining that He concerns Himself with only those "big moments" in your life . . . choice of college, career, mate, and so on? If so, you'd better think twice.

God's sovereign plans for you embrace a myriad of seemingly insignificant details. What a challenge to trust Him . . . to obey Him in everything . . . to walk in the closest fellowship with Him!

Believe me, the details count!

A Final Word

Rumors were flying around Jerusalem. Some of the women reported an empty tomb. Others spoke of visions and angels.

But these accounts only confused the two Emmaus disciples I mentioned earlier in the book. Had anybody actually *seen* Jesus? What could it all mean?

They hung around Jerusalem as long as they could, waiting for solid evidence. Finally, near the end of the day, the two men shrugged their shoulders, packed their duffle bags, and headed for home.

You know the story from there.

Jesus intruded into their lives on that homeward journey. He elbowed into their conversation, probing their thoughts, and pushing His point, "Did not the Christ have to suffer these things and then enter his glory?" (Luke 24:26).

The men listened intently, their hearts warmed by the words. They yearned to hear more, yet as they neared the village, "Jesus acted as if he were going farther" (v. 28). But they couldn't just let this Stranger walk off into the twilight. So they urged Him to stay, probably hoping to hear more of His startling perspective.

They all entered a room and sat down. Cleopas and his friend reclined at the table with this now-welcome Intruder, talking on and on. Someone placed bread before them. Someone else may have asked their Guest to give thanks. He did. A beautiful prayer. *But what was it about that voice? What was it about those strong hands? What was it about the way He broke bread? What did it remind them of? The crowd, the grass, the hillside, the baskets . . .* and suddenly "their eyes were opened and they recognized Him."

They were shocked. Stunned. This strange companion was the Lord Jesus Christ! How the tables had turned! Jesus had somehow become Host, and they the guests. *His* guests.

But they didn't have long to ponder their situation. As soon as the disciples recognized their risen Lord, "He disappeared from their sight."

What would you do at a time like that? The two men knew what to do. They didn't stand around, scratching their heads. The moment Jesus left them, even at that late hour, "They got up and returned at once to Jerusalem. There they found the Eleven and those with them assembled together" (v. 33) and the two told their story.

Can't you just imagine the scene? There they were, dusty, sweaty, gasping for breath, explaining it all to the Eleven. Suddenly their speech was interrupted by the Glorious Intruder Himself. "Peace be with you," Jesus said—and they just about jumped out of their skins. "They were startled and frightened, thinking they saw a ghost" (v. 37).

How were they to know Jesus had arrived ahead of them? Only a few hours before it was *Jesus* who had followed on the road to Emmaus; but somehow He had leaped ahead, waiting to spring His version of "Hello" on those who had followed *Him.*

What a change! Before, Jesus was the follower. Now, they followed Jesus. Once again the tables were turned.

Have the tables turned for you?

Perhaps in the past you've felt the Lord intrude, following after you, overstepping your comfort zones, grating against your self-will. You've sensed Him encroaching into your private time, invading, advancing, barging into areas you wish He'd ignore. You've heard His Spirit "talk out of turn," urging some inconvenient, untimely change in your habits, your schedule, your life. As Oswald Chambers says, "We resent what Jesus Christ reveals. But either Jesus Christ is the supreme authority on the human heart, or He is not worth paying attention to. Am I prepared to trust His penetration?"

Just as you're about to be irritated at this Intruder, something He says intrigues you. So let me ask . . . when Jesus intrudes into your life, how do you respond? Do you, like the disciples, feel your heart yearn for more? Do you call out to Him, urging Him, constraining Him to stay with you?

Or do you let Him pass by?

Ah, but if you would listen . . . if you would respond . . . if you would obey, you'd no longer consider the Lord an intruder. Instead you'd find yourself urging Him to stay, to tell you more, to reveal Himself further, to break bread at your table.

And when He does, you'll find that He does not stay put— He leads you on! Jesus will entice you to follow Him. Urge you to seek Him out. Allure you to go where He leads. You'll find yourself intruding into His mysteries, pleading with Him to explain more about His Word and Himself. You will follow Him, encroaching on the very throne room of heaven, setting up camp in the Holy of Holies.

I hope that somewhere, at some point in this book, God has broken bread with you, surprising you, revealing Himself in a personal way. I also hope you will sense the Lord Jesus leading you on, inviting you to follow.

Does God mind you intruding on Him? Well . . . "Ask and it will be given to you; seek and you will find; knock and the door will be opened to you. For everyone who asks receives. He who seeks find. And to him who knocks, the door will be opened" (Matthew 7:7-8).

So go ahead, ask. Go ahead, seek. Go ahead, knock. You can never intrude too much for God!

Other books by Joni Eareckson Tada:

Joni, 1976, Zondervan Publishing House
A Step Further, 1978, Zondervan Publishing House
All God's Children, 1981, Zondervan Publishing House
Choices . . . Changes, 1986, Zondervan Publishing House
Friendship Unlimited, 1987, Harold Shaw Publishers
Secret Strength, 1988, Multnomah Press

Children's books published by David C. Cook Publishing Co.:

Darcy, 1988
Jeremy, Barnabas, & the Wonderful Dream, 1987
Meet My Friends, 1987
Ryan and the Circus Wheels, 1988

Joni Eareckson Tada is founder and president of Joni and Friends, a Christian ministry that links the church with disabled people through evangelism, encouragement, and education.

If you or someone you know might benefit from the ministry of Joni and Friends, you may write her at:

Joni and Friends
P.O. Box 3333
Agoura Hills, CA 91301

Chapter 1

1. Oswald Chambers, *My Utmost for His Highest* (New York: Dodd, Mead & Co., Inc., 1935), p. 202.

2. C. S. Lewis, *The Weight of Glory* (Grand Rapids: William B. Eerdmans Publishing Co., 1949), p. 13.

Chapter 3

3. Andrew Murray, *With Christ in the School of Prayer* (Old Tappan, N.J.: Fleming H. Revell Co., 1953).

4. Philip Yancey, "God's Not Fair (and I'm Glad He Isn't)," *Christianity Today*, November 20, 1987, p. 72.

Chapter 4

5. Rev. Gregory Hotchkiss, "Their Eyes Were Opened," *Episcopal Recorder*, March 1988, 3d series, vol. 1, no. 6, p. 3.

6. J. I. Packer, *Hot Tub Religion* (Wheaton, Ill.: Tyndale House Publishers, Inc., 1987), p. 192-193.

7. Bishop J. C. Ryle, *Holiness* (Cambridge: James Clarke and Co., Inc., 1964), p. 183.

Chapter 8

8. Peter Kreeft, *Making Sense Out of Suffering* (Ann Arbor, Mich.: Servant Books, 1986), p. 143.

SCRIPTURE
INDEX